Sawtooth

New Quilts from an Old Favorite

edited by **Linda Baxter Lasco**

American Quilter's Society

P. O. Box 3290 • Paducah, KY 42002-3290

www.AmericanQuilter.com

THANK YOU SPONSORS

Clover

※ **Fairfield**
Quality Polyester Products for Home and Industry

JANOME
Because You Simply Love To Sew™

The American Quilter's Society (AQS), located in Paducah, Kentucky, is dedicated to promoting the accomplishments of today's quilters. Through its publications and events, AQS strives to honor today's quiltmakers and their work and to inspire future creativity and innovation in quiltmaking.

Text © 2008, American Quilter's Society
Artwork © 2008 American Quilter's Society

Executive Editor: Nicole C. Chambers
Editor: Linda Baxter Lasco
Graphic Design: Lynda Smith
Cover Design: Michael Buckingham
Photography: Charles R. Lynch

American Quilterís Society
P. O. Box 3290 ï Paducah, KY 42002-3290
www.americanquilter.com

Additional copies of this book may be ordered from the American Quilter's Society, PO Box 3290, Paducah, KY 42002-3290, or online at: www.AmericanQuilter.com.

Attention Photocopying Service: Please note the following—publisher and author give permission to photocopy pages 24, 25, 40, 81, 90, 91, 92 for personal use only.

Library of Congress Cataloging-in-Publication Data

Sawtooth : new quilts from an old favorite / by American Quilter's Society.
    p. cm.
  ISBN 978-1-57432-960-5
  1. Patchwork--Patterns. 2. Quilting--Patterns. 3. Patchwork quilts--United States--History. I. American Quilter's Society.

TT835.S2765 2008
746.46'041--dc22

                                              2008009368

Proudly printed and bound in the
United States of America

DEDICATION

The National Quilt Museum, Museum of the American Quilter's Society, has created this contest to recognize and share with others the fascinating variety of interpretations that quilters bring forth from a single traditional quilt pattern. This book is dedicated to all those who see a traditional quilt block and can visualize both its link to the past and its bridge to the future.

National Quilt Museum
The Museum of the American Quilter's Society

"Honoring Today's Quilter"

The Museum of the American Quilter's Society, MAQS, is an exciting place where the public can learn more about quilts, quiltmaking and quiltmakers, and experience quilts that inspire and delight.

The museum celebrates today's quilts and quiltmakers through exhibits of quilts from the museum's collection and selected temporary exhibits. By providing a variety of workshops and other programs, MAQS helps to encourage, inspire, and enhance the development of today's quilter.

Whether presenting new or antique quilts, the museum promotes understanding of and respect for all quilts—new and antique, traditional and innovative, machine made and handmade, utility and art.

CONTENTS

PREFACE

While preservation of the past is one of a museum's primary functions, its greatest service is performed as it links the past to the present and to the future. With that intention, the Museum of the American Quilter's Society sponsors an annual contest and exhibit called New Quilts from an Old Favorite.

Created to acknowledge our quiltmaking heritage and to recognize innovation, creativity, and excellence, the contest challenges today's quiltmakers to interpret a single traditional quilt block in a work of their own design. Each year contestants respond with a myriad of stunning interpretations.

Sawtooth: New Quilts from an Old Favorite is a wonderful representation of these interpretations. You'll find a brief description of the 2008 contest, followed by a presentation of the five award winners and the 13 finalists and their quilts.

Full-color photographs of the quilts accompany each quiltmaker's comments—comments that provide insight into their widely diverse creative processes. Full-size patterns for the traditional Sawtooth block are included to form the basis for your own rendition. Tips, techniques, and patterns contributed by the contestants offer an artistic framework for your own work.

Our wish is that *Sawtooth: New Quilts from an Old Favorite* will further our quiltmaking heritage as new quilts based on the Sawtooth block are inspired by the outstanding quilts, patterns, and instructions in this book.

THE CONTEST

Although the contest encouraged unconventional creativity, there were some basic requirements for entries:

- Quilts entered in the contest were to be recognizable in some way as being related to the Sawtooth block.
- The finished size of the quilt was to be a minimum of 50" in width and height but could not exceed 80" in any one dimension.
- Quilting was required on each quilt entered in the contest.
- A quilt could be entered only by the person(s) who made it.
- Each entry must have been completed after December 31, 2004.

To enter the contest, each quiltmaker was asked to submit an entry form and two slides or digital images of their quilt—one of the full quilt and a second of a detail from the piece. Quiltmakers from around the world responded to the challenge of using this traditional block in non-traditional ways.

Three jurors viewed dozens of slides, deliberating over design, use of materials, interpretation of the theme, and technical excellence. Eventually they narrowed the field of entries to 18 finalists and the quiltmakers were invited to submit their quilts for judging.

With the finalists' quilts at hand, three judges meticulously examined the pieces, evaluating them again for design, innovation, theme, and workmanship. First- through fifth-place award winners were selected and notified.

Each year the New Quilts from an Old Favorite contest winners and finalists are featured in an exhibit that opens at the Museum of the American Quilter's Society in Paducah, Kentucky. Over a two-year period, the exhibit travels to a number of museums across North America and is viewed by thousands of quilt enthusiasts. Corporate sponsorship of the contest helps to underwrite costs, enabling even smaller museums across the country to host the exhibit.

Annually, the contest winners and finalists are included in a beautiful book published by the American Quilter's Society. *Sawtooth: New Quilts from an Old Favorite* is the fifteenth in the contest, exhibit, and publication series. It joins the following other traditional block designs used as contest themes: Rose of Sharon, Dresden Plate, Seven Sisters, Monkey Wrench, Feathered Star, Tumbling Blocks, Bear's Paw, Storm at Sea, Kaleidoscope, Pineapple, Mariner's Compass, Ohio Star, Log Cabin, and Double Wedding Ring.

The current contest block is Burgoyne Surrounded (2009). Future contest blocks include Sunflower (2010), Orange Peel (2011), and Baskets (2012).

For information about entering the current year's contest, write to Museum of the American Quilter's Society at PO Box 1540, Paducah, KY 42002-1540; call (270) 442-8856; or visit MAQS online at www.quiltmuseum.org.

THE SAWTOOTH BLOCK

In the development of quilt styles in the United States, quilts made of a single repeated block became the predominant form around the middle of the nineteenth century. What we consider the quintessential American quilt came about after a long progression from wholecloth to medallion to block-style. Most Sawtooth quilts fall into this category of block-style quilts. However, there are examples of borders and overall quilt designs designated as Sawtooth.

What exactly is a Sawtooth block design? All include triangles, usually half-square triangles, representing the teeth on a saw blade. There are ten different patterns by this name in quilt historian Barbara Brackman's *Encyclopedia of Pieced Quilt Patterns*. These patterns date from perhaps 1884, when *Farm and Fireside* began publishing quilt patterns, until 1978 as found in *The Quiltmaker's Handbook* by Michael James. Another pattern is named Saw Tooth and yet another as Saw Teeth. Brackman lists 14 designs as being "Misc. Sawtooth Types," including Waves of the Sea, Delectable Mountains, and Large Star, found in the *Ladies Home Journal* of 1896. Many of the Sawtooth patterns listed in the encyclopedia were published during the 1930s. This is not surprising as this was the first major quilt revival after the Civil War and many pattern designers of the time syndicated their designs.

There are numerous examples of nineteenth-century Sawtooth block quilts that may have inspired later quilters. The *Quilts of Tennessee* survey documents Mary B. Few's solid red and white 1850–1875 Sawtooth quilt. Two other quilts from that documentation project, one in solids by Mary E. Barnes of Cowan, Tennessee, and a navy print and white quilt by Melinda Graves Heath of the Walnut Grove area in Tennessee, date from 1875 to 1900. The former is actually a Pickle Dish variation pattern but the family calls it Sawtooth. The Tennessee survey also includes a scrap Double Sawtooth quilt made by an unknown quilter in the 1880s. A Sawtooth quilt in the collection of the Great Lakes Quilt Center was pieced in 1876 by Matilda Vary of Ceresco, Calhoun County, Michigan, from an array of print fabrics; it was finished by others over a hundred years later. The Kentucky Quilt Project documents a Sawtooth quilt top of four prints made between 1850 and 1875 by Nancy Milan Grinter of Logan County, Kentucky, and one of scrap fabrics and cochineal print sashing made by Alice Brown of Wayne County, Kentucky, during that same period. A very unusual block resembling a circular saw that was used for a quilt made by Elizabeth Ogden of New Castle, Kentucky, before 1800 is titled Saw Tooth Moon. It is pieced of white and a dark blue print.

Center Diamond Amish quilts sometimes have each large square edged by Sawtooth borders. These quilts are particularly bold; Jonathan Holstein collected several. He and Gail van der Hoof included a Sawtooth medallion-style quilt in the seminal 1971 exhibit at the Whitney Museum of American Art, Abstract Design in American Quilts. It was of red and off-white solid fabrics and dates from 1890 to 1910.

For today's quilters, Sawtooth typically brings to mind an outer border of half-square triangles. These are found on quilts as far back as the late eighteenth century, and many early medallion quilts featured interior Sawtooth borders as design elements. These Sawtooth borders were sometimes appliquéd as a long single strip of fabric instead of being pieced of individual triangles. The Round Robin quilt craze and the many books on quilt border designs and solutions of the 1990s cemented the concept in the minds of today's quilters that Sawtooth refers to a border instead of a block.

Sawtooth quilts of the past were pieced of solids and prints, sometimes with a scrappy look, sometimes very orderly. The jagged points of the pieced triangles lent energy to the overall quilt design that must have appealed to many quiltmakers of the past. Today's quiltmakers are no different and they have exploited the possibilities of the design, curving and twisting the elements or building an orderly structure for manipulating color. The imaginations of the quilt artists of today honor the traditional Sawtooth quilts of the past and their makers.

My thanks to the Quilt Index, found online at www.quiltindex .org, the Great Lakes Quilt Center online collections at museum .msu.edu/glqc/index.html, and the International Quilt Study Center's online collections at www.quiltstudy.org.

Judy Schwender
Curator of Collections and Registrar
Museum of the American Quilter's Society

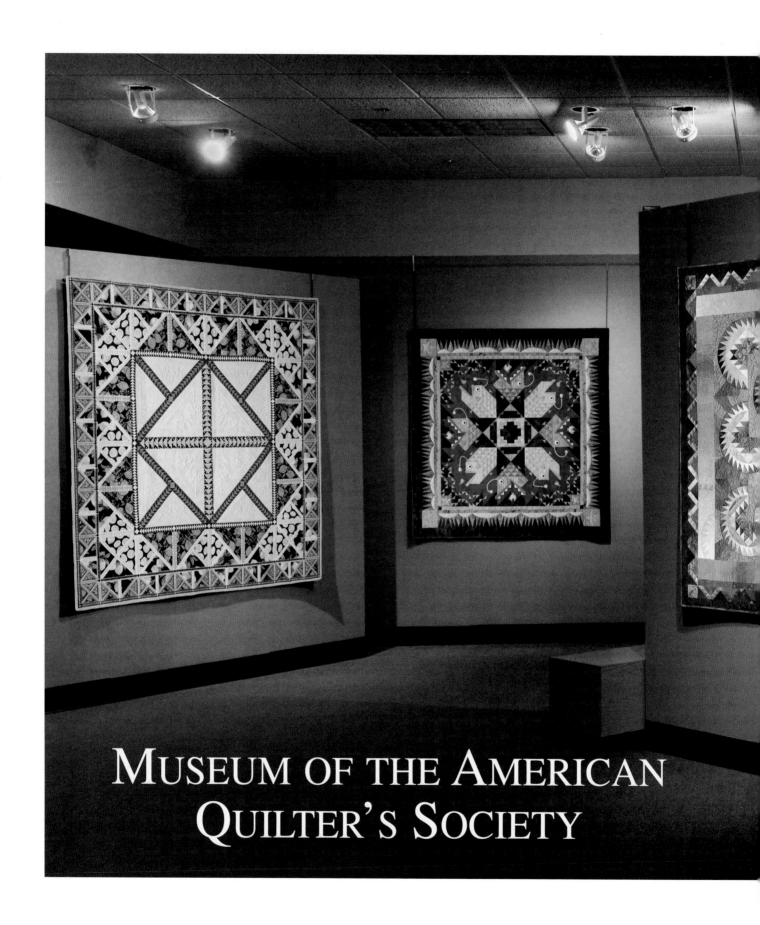

MUSEUM OF THE AMERICAN
QUILTER'S SOCIETY

215 Jefferson Street • Paducah, Kentucky 42001 • www.quiltmuseum.org • (270) 442-8856

First Place
Claudia Clark Myers
& Marilyn Badger

Claudia Clark Myers

I attended my first quilt show in 1991 and was dumbfounded by the creativity and variety of the quilts I saw there. Ever since, I have enjoyed the luxury of seeing designs in my mind come to life as quilts. My inspirations come from within but, like putting treasures into a safety deposit box, they have been saved up from visuals that have been stuffed into my mind—works of art, other quilts, gardens, classes I have taken, places I have been, costumes, and color, color, color.

Working with Marilyn is a joy. I trust her completely. I always know that my designs will be skillfully quilted, with many hours of thought going into the quilting designs that will enhance them. We share pride in our quilts because we have both put our best into them.

Marilyn Badger

My interest in quiltmaking began in 1978 when my husband and I lived on our boat in Marina Del Rey, California. I subscribed to *Quilter's Newsletter Magazine* and was hooked. My first quilt was a king-size Lone Star quilt that I pieced by hand—not a brilliant choice for a beginner!

Quilting has been a way of life since purchasing my first longarm machine in 1991. I have taught longarm classes for 11 years in my studio, as well as in various cities across the United States, Canada, Australia, and Japan. My husband and I have been in the longarm accessory business since 1996. I have served as a consultant to APQS, representing them at major quilt shows throughout the year.

I always look forward to receiving a new project from Claudia. Each one requires new techniques and designs that keep me on my toes as a machine quilter. Another truly amazing quilt artist who has been a tremendous inspiration to me is Caryl Bryer Fallert. She has been a blessing to machine quilters everywhere!

The future of quilting is difficult to predict and I pretty much focus on today, but I'm hopeful that Claudia and I can continue our quilting adventures for many years to come.

Claudia & Marilyn's photo by Hartley B. Badger

BERRY PATCH 70" x 70"

When I start to work, the ideas come tumbling out
like the clowns stuffed into a tiny car in a circus act! Claudia

Fig. 1.

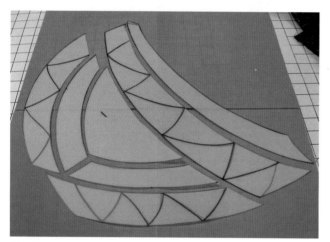

Fig. 2.

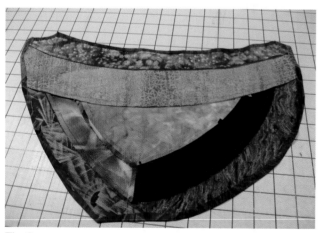

Fig. 3.

Fig. 4.

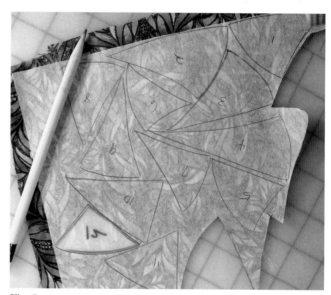

Fig. 5.

Fig. 6.

Inspiration & Design

Claudia

I thought I had a great idea for a quilt to enter in the MAQS Sawtooth Contest this year. Actually, I sketched it while waiting for my plane after the Nashville AQS Quilt Expo. I had purchased a great piece of over-dyed dragon fabric from Wendy Richardson, and it was inspiring me. When I got home, I started putting together fabrics, drafting the blocks on graph paper, making templates—all the things you do when you are flying on the wings of enthusiasm for a new quilt. Then I started paper piecing the blocks and putting them up on my design wall. I realized, after three days of working, that—I HATED it!

Marilyn and I had already decided to make a quilt together for this contest, so I couldn't just quit. I had to start over. In a frenzy, I decided to make a free-form drawing (fig. 1), abstracting the Sawtooth block and making it life-size, so I could cut it apart and use it as templates for my curved piecing (fig. 2). When I put it up on the design wall, it either looked like tropical leaves, or (horrors!) a huge spider. To reinforce the tropical plant idea and get away from the wildlife, I added enormous, juicy berries (or pumpkins, as some have said).

After all this changing of my mind, there wasn't a lot of time left for intricate precision piecing of points. So I put together the large curves of the leaves (figs. 3–4), and using numbered plastic patterns, I cut (fig. 5), fused (fig. 6), and satin-stitched the odd-shaped points onto the curved leaf bases (fig. 7). The berries were pieced and machine embroidered and then the whole thing was appliquéd onto the background (fig. 8). I used the wonderful over-dyed dragon fabric in the border and drafted another, more traditional, Sawtooth block to sprinkle around on the edges that was "fat" and reminded me of the berries (fig. 9). I then turned it all over to Marilyn to do her magic.

Fig. 7.

Fig. 8.

Fig. 9.

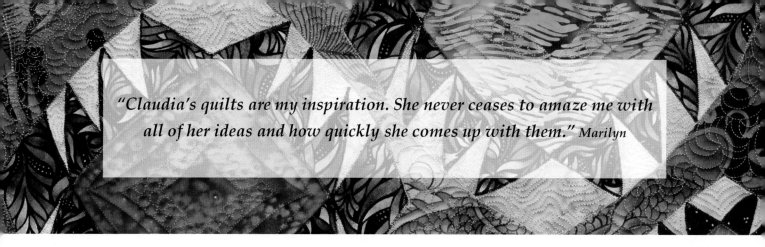

Marilyn

When I received BERRY PATCH from Claudia, I had two weeks to complete the quilting, attach the sleeve and binding, photograph it, and get the entry in the mail before leaving for Houston and the International Quilt Festival. Nothing like a pressure deadline to get something done! Luckily I had photos that Claudia had e-mailed to me at various stages and I had been planning the quilting designs prior to receiving the quilt (fig. 10).

I like to carry some of the design elements of the quilt into the quilting, so I made drawings of Claudia's various Sawtooth blocks and used them as quilting motifs. These were marked with chalk then stitched (fig. 11).

I used Superior Brytes™, my Color Concepts, and Highlights™ thread, Madeira Polyneon thread, and Fairfield Soft Touch® cotton batting.

I wanted to create a unique background filler other than stippling or designs I had previously used on other quilts. I did drawings on paper and then stitched them out on a sample piece of fabric before actually putting the quilt on the machine (figs. 12–14). I always like to practice a new design beforehand to make sure it transitions well from drawing to quilting. What may look good on paper might not work out so well in actual quilting. I wanted to have some of the leaves floating around in the background, but after quilting they didn't show up as much as I liked.

At this point we decided Claudia would paint them. So BERRY PATCH was overnighted to her for the painting and photography the next day. Our entry went into the mailbox the day before leaving for Houston!

Fig. 10.

Fig. 11.

Fig. 12.

Fig. 13.

Fig. 14.

Ann's photo by Jessica Horton

Second Place
Ann Horton

I suppose it all started with growing up on the farm. We produced and preserved practically everything! Grandpa was the gardener and I loved to follow him around the farm, interested in all the growing things. Our farm teemed with life—kittens in the hayloft, baby ducks and chicks in the spring, a baby calf every couple years, rabbits, wildlife—it was all part of my daily experience. Then there was the farmhouse "women's work." Cooking, canning—we used what we had and made it work in wonderful ways. Sewing was a regular part of life. My grandma made quilts from feedsacks, my mom made my clothes, and I sewed for my dolls and later for myself. My mom sewed on an old treadle machine and I learned on that, too.

When I was ten, my father came home from town with an electric sewing machine and soon I took it over, sewing on any cloth I could locate. I remember making a dress and matching shorts out of an old, not quite white bed sheet! Our family motto of "just DO it, and do it with what you have on hand" has propelled me through life with an eye towards originality. I have always designed my own quilts and while my amazing fabric stash makes "doing it with what I have on hand" a bit of a stretch of my original farmhouse philosophy, it certainly does justify adding a bit more fabric when I happen upon it.

Music and quilt art share a sweet dance in my life. As a musician I share the excitement of voice and song with my fellow musicians and as a quilter I share creativity and the passion of art with my best friends. I am richly blessed to have the opportunity and freedom to explore the bounty of possibilities in both realms. I often hear how a quilt will "sing" and how music "weaves the notes together." At quilt retreats, my sisters-of-the-cloth and I often sit together and sing as we work. The simplicity and beauty of that shared grace in stitch and song reflect the depth of emotion with which I approach my art.

Living a country life in the constant beauty of northern California's coastal mountains, I am daily inspired by the spin of life around me. From the smallest insects to the biggest bears, I am always excited to see what bit of creation is waiting to be discovered. My quilts reflect this love with a myriad of colors, shapes, and stories to tell. There are always more stories to tell as well as more quilts to make. My approach is to embrace the learning curve and use the best machine I can afford. My ideas evolve rapidly and I rely on my equipment to keep up with the flow!

WEB OF LIFE 77" x 77"

New fabrics, textures, threads, designs and embellishments—it is all an enticing journey calling me to plunge in and see where the next quilt will take me. Additionally, ever expanding technology provides challenges and solutions in my quilting studio.

Fig. 1.

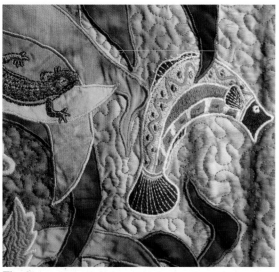

Fig. 2.

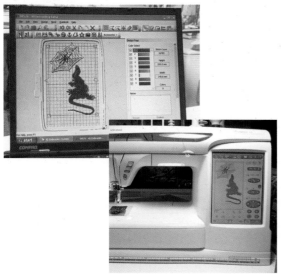

Figs. 3–4.

Inspiration & Design

WEB OF LIFE was an extraordinarily fun quilt to make. The name says it all for me—a story quilt of the diversity and richness of interwoven life in a rainforest. Inspired by the colorful images of Central American flora and fauna, I could not resist translating this cradle of life into fabric art. The quilt was meant to be a showcase for embroidery and that is where the fun began.

First, though, I had to start with the Sawtooth blocks. Begun some eight years ago, the pattern was sketched from a tattered scrap of an antique quilt I found at an estate sale. The pattern looked like a spider web to me and I eagerly cut triangles to piece from my little paper sketches. After making seven blocks, however, I became discouraged by the assorted calico background triangles I had used. Unhappily, I put the whole project away.

When the Sawtooth block was announced for the NQOF contest, I remembered the blocks and began again. Replacing the background with a vibrant mottled green did the trick. Now my spider web was looking decidedly jungle-like and I was ready to design my river border. Expanding partial blocks into the border to reinforce the interwoven effect, I added the blue batik and blue-green print and pulled out all the stops on extravagant machine appliqué and embroidery.

I am fortunate to own a large library of digitized embroidery designs and I am careful with my selections. Nature motifs appeal to me, and for this quilt I selected designs from a dozen or more different collections. My first selection was a set of digitized appliqué designs called Hola Mola by Nancy Vasilchik. The playful parrots (fig. 1) set the stage for all the rest of the border designs. Lizards, tropical flowers, frogs, fish (fig. 2), turtles, insects, butterflies, and, of course, the spider, all found their place in a rousing interplay of activity in the rainforest border. Freehand cut appliqué leaves and branches form the setting for the jungle life to interact, and interact it does.

Technique – Digitized Machine Embroidery

I have made many quilts with machine embroidery, but this quilt represents an advanced exploration of software and technology for me. For a number of years I sewed on a simple sewing and embroidery machine and did not use software.

Several years ago, after gaining recognition in an international art quilt contest, I won a top-end machine and the software to make the perfect combination. In WEB OF LIFE, I found myself utilizing my Husqvarna embroidery software to great effect. Loading the designs on my computer (fig. 3), I would happily resize and reshape the images, combine them, and when satisfied, send them directly to my Husqvarna Designer SE machine via a cable connection (fig. 4). Having the computer software program interfaced with my computerized machine was marvelous! Once the design was on the machine, I could still do the final minute adjustments to fit the design perfectly onto the leaves and branches in the border (fig. 5).

I cannot emphasize enough how amazing and exciting the use of software is in this process. Prior to obtaining my software program, I made my quilts directly from the design with limited ability to change the size. In those days, hooping and placement were painstaking. Now, with the software, the sky is the limit for design possibilities. In this quilt, I was able to use many different types of embroidery and alter the designs in the software to work together in the quilt. Magic! My freehand leaves and branches were fused onto the river background with a mind towards space for the addition of flowers, fruit, and creatures. My machine allowed me to carefully settle the embroideries onto the leaves with precision, adding to the realistic dimension of the quilt.

Fig. 5.

When it was time for quilting inside those green setting triangles, I again looked to my digitized designs and software for a creative solution. A lovely botanical moth was resized and shaped to fit into the triangles with beautiful quilting detail (fig. 6).

And so WEB OF LIFE unfolds—the lizard eyes the insect (fig. 7), and the parrot anxiously watches the caterpillar while the frog floats nearby (fig. 8). Lush fruit entices the toucan and the spider weaves her web to catch the next passing victim. Throughout the jungle the exotic, multicolored lizards find their home above the river that teems with fish, snakes, and other creatures (fig. 9). Truly this quilt celebrates life and the connections between all living things.

Fig. 6.

Fig. 7.

Fig. 8.

Fig. 9.

Ann's photo by Casey Sanderson

Third Place
Ann L. Petersen

I have been around quilting and quilters my whole life. Both of my grandmothers passed on lovely quilts to me but it was my father's mother, Bessie Lucore, who was the true quilting enthusiast. She was a rancher's wife in humble circumstances who worked long hard days and raised four children to adulthood, but every day she found time for quilting. She was expert enough to take in quilt tops from around the country and quilt them for other people for a little extra money, but working on her own quilts was her joy.

Unfortunately, my grandmother died shortly after I married and I never got the chance to go learn quilting at her knee. So in 1973 I enrolled in a quilting class where I was taught "new" techniques, such as using lids from margarine containers for templates instead of cardboard. After my son was born in 1980, I decided to go into the business of making nursery items to help support my sewing hobby. I called my business Nursery Niceties and over the next 10 years made many baby quilts, almost all appliquéd. In the late 1980s Eleanor Burns began to appear on my local public television station and I was fascinated with her strip-piecing techniques. Before long I rediscovered a passion for traditional patchwork.

In 1997 I noticed a sign at my local quilt store, looking for new employees. I quickly applied and started to work there in August. I am extremely fortunate that not only is the Great American Quilt Factory my local store, it is also the home of Possibilities, a quilt book publisher. I now work there full-time as a designer.

My husband and I have been married for 36 years and are looking forward to retirement. After living in Colorado for almost my entire life, we may decide to live part-time in the Phoenix, Arizona, area where our son and daughter-in-law reside.

Inspiration & Design

The infinite possibilities of simple geometric shapes and vibrant color combinations are the inspiration that spurs me on to the next quilt. I have played with many art and craft techniques over the years, but the palette that quilting offers seems to me to be the richest one offered in all of the artistic areas. Not only is there fabric in every color of the rainbow, but also when you start to combine the many prints available, you get a glorious effect. Then the quilting is added, giving texture and sculptural qualities to the quilt beyond the visual texture from the fabric.

CARMELIZED SAWBLADES 59" x 70"

My grandmother, Bessie Lucore, was a "real quilter" if there ever was one and I know she would have enthusiastically supported all the machine work I am privileged to do today.

Fig. 1. Paper-pieced blocks

Fig. 2. S-curve from the upper-right corner of the full quilt

Fig. 3. Light-to-dark gradation from the center of the quilt

I have followed the New Quilts from an Old Favorite Contest for a number of years and designed quilts to enter a couple of times, but never managed to get one made in time for the contest deadline. Last spring I began to put several designs on graph paper. Then, while in Paducah for the AQS Quilt Show & Contest, I saw a gorgeous over-dyed decorator fabric in Wendy Richardson's booth that I knew would be my inspiration for my Sawtooth quilt. The fabric has fine line drawings of apples and other fruit and is over-dyed with golden yellows, oranges, reds, and even a small amount of teal. I also purchased some rayon cording dyed in the same colors.

Technique

In mid-September I sat down to start my quilt. I had drawn a design consisting of four quadrants, each with a different setting of Sawtooth blocks. I selected the simplest one and started to sew it using my over-dyed fabric as the background and a series of shades of brown from dark to light for each consecutive block. I discovered that the heavier weight of the decorator fabric made my piecing unsatisfactory and I quickly abandoned this idea. One of the quadrant designs was a take-off on the Card Trick block, and I decided to use this design for the entire quilt. After several hours of figuring out the math involved, I began to piece my half-square triangle units.

After piecing nearly all of them, each in a different shade, I discovered that I had forgotten to add seam allowances on the unit dimensions. At this point I began to put all the fabrics and ideas away, certain I had once again run out of time. As I was folding up my design sketches, I noticed a quick, small drawing on the back of the paper for a Sawtooth block in a circle. In just a few minutes, I figured out a paper-piecing pattern for the block that would work easily (fig. 1). Suddenly, I was sewing blocks that were pleasing and fun. The outside piece of the block was cut oversized so that I could play with my setting and get the S-curves to form when two blocks came together (fig. 2).

For each block I picked one of the colors in my inspiration fabric and used it for the half-square triangles in the circle. Each block's pieces were graded dark to light so that when three blocks in one color family were set together, the color variegated from dark to light and back again (fig. 3).

After the circles were pieced, I felt they needed a little more definition. Couching the hand-dyed rayon cording along the seam line with a fine red thread between the circles and background was the answer (fig. 4). Doing this before sewing the blocks together meant that I did not have to worry about finishing the ends of the cording. I decided to reinforce the Sawtooth theme with a border made up of half-Sawtooth blocks (fig. 5).

I quilted by almost thread painting partial-block designs from the center. I made a plastic template by tracing the block design and cutting out channels to draw the piecing lines. Then I used the template over and over to draw partial blocks throughout the wide border. I quilted it heavily with a decorative thread to color the different areas of the block. While this made good blocks, it also flattened the quilted areas while leaving the background looking quite puffy. Not the effect I wanted. This meant I needed to flatten the background as well.

The last part of the quilt to be quilted was the background area of dark tan wedges. Since there was a small amount of teal in the couched cording, I decided to use a variegated teal polyester thread for freeform feathers to fill in the area (fig. 6).

I often start my quilting in the border. I have discovered that it keeps the piecing lines straight before twisting and pulling the quilt through the bed of the machine has a chance to distort them. It also tends to flatten a large area of the quilt, making handling the center of the quilt easier. When doing CARMELIZED SAWBLADES, quilting the thread-painted border first also meant that I had done the area with the densest quilting first. Then I could match the density in the rest of the quilting to the border so that the quilt would lie flat.

I drew the block pattern on tracing paper placed on top of a piece of circular graph paper. My circular graph paper came Barbara Barber's book *Foolproof Curves: Quilts with Bias Strips and Continuous Paper Piecing*. The outer curved, spiked ring, the center section, and the background piece were drawn out separately and seam allowances were added to each. The background section was drawn oversize and cut down once the blocks were made to the size I needed for my setting.

Fig. 4. Couching along the seam line

Fig. 5. Half-Sawtooth blacks in the borders

Fig. 6. Freeform feathers

I pieced the curved ring first with the colored triangles to the outside of the ring.

Start at one end and label it light; each ring will take 8 colored triangles and 8 off-white to tan triangles. I usually picked 10 of each color so that when the rings were pieced together, the two light (or dark) pieces that fall next to each other were not the same fabric, though maybe of the same value. These fabrics were sorted in a light-to-dark gradation. I cut strips of each fabric that were approximately 3" wide and pieced the triangles directly from the strips. When making the second block in a colorway, I made sure that the light-to-dark gradation continued from one block to the next. I made a total of six blocks in each colorway.

The center units of the blocks were pieced starting with the triangle strip. Pieces numbered 3, 5, and 7 were a color; while pieces 1, 2, 4, 6, and 8 were off-white to tan, each piece of a different fabric. I used $2^{1}/_{2}$" squares cut in half once on the diagonal for these pieces. I used $4^{1}/_{2}$" squares of the over-dyed decorator fabric (my inspiration piece) cut in half once on the diagonal for the center triangle. I used a 3" x 9" piece of whichever print I liked for the outer curved piece, then trimmed the finished section.

The curved ring and center units were joined along the curved edge. I start by finding the center of each piece and matching those, pin match the edges, then ease the rest of the curve together using a pin every $^{1}/_{2}$" or so. It seems to me to be easier to use a lot of pins when the paper is on the fabric and there are a lot of seam lines to deal with.

I put all these units on the design wall. I divided the tan to brown fabrics I wanted to use for the backgrounds into three piles by value—lightest, medium, and darkest. The backgrounds were pieced with the lightest values in the center and the darkest along the outside edge of the quilt top. The background units were joined to the center units in the same manner described above. Once I had all the blocks sewn into complete blocks, I could match the two sets of blocks that needed to have their center strips form a continuous line and trim the outside of the background that was in excess. Then I trimmed all of the blocks down to the same size and sewed them together.

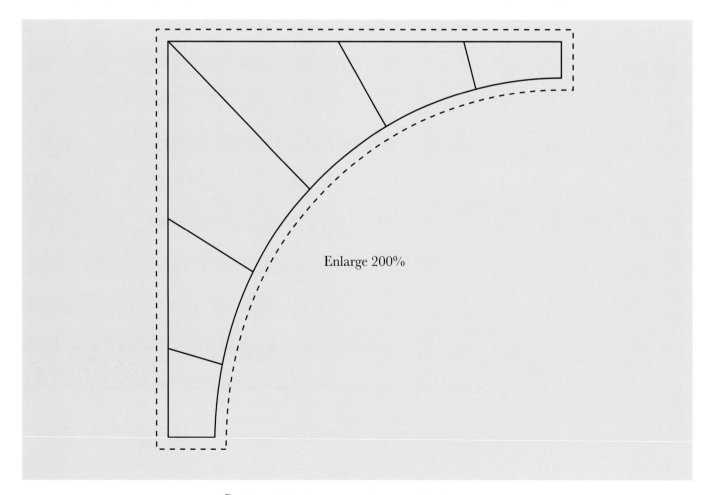

Enlarge 200%

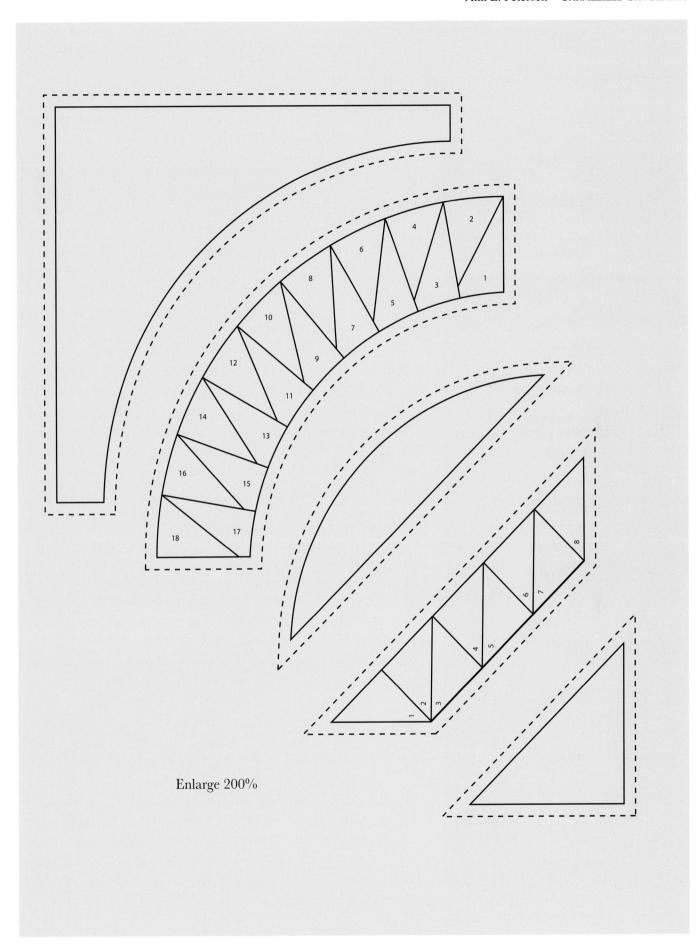

Enlarge 200%

Fourth Place
Jill H. Bryant & Nancy S. Brown

Nancy S. Brown

I started making quilts almost 20 years ago after my mother took a quilting class and taught me what she had learned. I had always enjoyed drawing and doing all sorts of crafts so I thought I would try a quilt. I planned to make one quilt just for fun but I soon got hooked. I have always loved animals and found that by using appliqué and a variety of the wonderful fabric prints available I could create unique yet realistic animal portraits. I do hand appliqué because I like both the process and the results. I have made many animal quilts but with the wide variety of subjects available I feel there are many more waiting to be made.

I was never very fond of piecing until I discovered foundation piecing a few years ago. Now I like to incorporate it in the backgrounds and borders of my animal quilts. However, the museum contest was a bit of a challenge for me since the Sawtooth is a pieced block and there wasn't a lot of room for appliqué. It has been a fun experience. Since I worked with a good friend, I got to do something a little more whimsical and brighter than usual.

Jill H. Bryant

Like so many quilters, I have sewn since I was young. It wasn't until I joined a guild that I discovered true quilting. I have been hooked ever since and the obsession has grown. I love trying new things and often fail but I learn as I go, which is even more fun. I love the MAQS contest because it gets me to think outside the box and try to create something new. I rarely follow a pattern. I would like to sometimes but nope, I seem to do it the hard way and trudge forward, creating as I go. I wish I could find a style but that hasn't happened yet. I love everything about color and construction and maybe, someday soon, I will have a style of my own.

Nancy and I met some years ago in Paducah when she placed in both the New Quilts from an Old Favorite contest and in the AQS Quilt Show & Contest. I walked up to her, introduced myself and said, "I hate you." Nothing personal and she didn't take it that way, thank goodness. I complimented her on her work, which I love, and the meeting passed. The following year, I came across Nancy again. I went up and asked, "Do you remember me?" Her reply, "Yes, you're the one who hates me." We've been friends ever since.

Jill & Nancy's photo by Nancy S. Brown and Linda Gruber

BEYOND THE SEA 55" x 55"

I make animal quilts because I feel that animals are an important part of this world and should be celebrated and preserved. Nancy

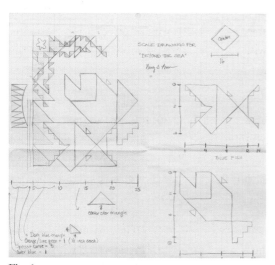

Fig. 1.

Fig. 2.

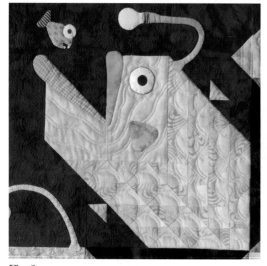

Fig. 3.

Inspiration & Design

Nancy

It wasn't until a few years ago that Jill and I decided it might be fun to make a quilt together for the museum contest. We thought about it for a couple of years but the timing or the block never seemed right for us. This year we decided to go for it. Since I really love animals, Jill agreed to do something with an animal theme and came up with the fish theme. We both wanted it to be bright and whimsical and we both worked on designs.

I have been fascinated with the unusual glowing fish with big eyes and big teeth found deep in the sea ever since I had a picture book about them when I was child. These fish can create their own light using a process called bioluminescence and I always just thought they looked like they had light bulbs on their heads. So I decided to design a medallion-style quilt inspired by these fish but making them much more colorful than they really are, putting actual light bulbs on their heads. I added the little appliqué fish to add some curves to soften all the straight lines. Jill came up with the great spiky sea anemone border that really makes the quilt come together.

I used graph paper to design the center part of the quilt. I knew I wanted two kinds of deep sea fish—one with big teeth and the other a little calmer. Half-square triangles would be incorporated in the teeth, scales, fins, and tails (fig. 1). I wanted a repeating, symmetrical design, so I started by dividing it into quarters and placing one blue fish in each section, then placing the orange and yellow fish in between the blue with the tails interlocking. I was pleased to see an Ohio Star form between the fish and accentuated it with the darkest blue color. I added a dark blue Sawtooth around the outside to balance the star. I thought the corners needed something and added the green half-square triangles to suggest seaweed. The little fish were added later. Jill added the sea anemone border design.

Techniques

Nancy

I did a line drawing first on the graph paper, and I thought I would color it in so Jill could get the general idea of what I was thinking and we could work out the actual colors later. I used the few colored pencils that I had and colored the fish yellow, orange, and turquoise (fig. 2). When it came time to choose the actual colors, we both decided that we liked those colors the best. Serendipity played a big role in color choice.

As much as I liked the border, I thought there was absolutely no way I could ever piece such skinny little spikes. Then Jill said, "Why don't you do the border and the appliqué and I will piece the center?" I think Jill suffered more piecing my silly fish with all the triangles (fig. 3). (And boy oh boy, did I hear about it! Hey, I'm an appliquér. The piecing didn't look so bad on graph paper.) I don't think I realized how small the pieces were until I saw the actual top.

So I did the appliqué and pieced the sea anemone border and Jill pieced the center. Jill likes to use starch on the fabrics to keep them crisp. I found that I have an allergic reaction to starch and had to wash it out whenever I got the quilt. By using a tearaway interfacing for my foundation piecing (and leaving it in), it had a similar effect to the starch in keeping my sections crisp and stabilized—and I think it made Jill happy.

Jill did all the fabulous machine quilting, designing all the patterns and adding a lot of great details that really enhance the design. I think in the end we made a good team. Our skills complemented each other and the friendship remained intact.

Jill

Nancy sent me her original design and I redrafted it, full size. I had already sent her the borders to be foundation pieced and I lived with the nightmare that I might end up piecing the center incorrectly. When I foundation piece, I take one 8" x 11" piece of graph paper and draw all the lines needed. Then, I only have to copy it and cut it apart on the lines. Anyone looking at this pattern would say I'm nuts and I would agree with them (fig. 4). Nancy thought those dark Sawtooth triangles made a good design element, but it was a piecing nightmare for me. (Love you, Nancy!)

Dividing the pattern into four exact quadrants helped *tremendously* with the piecing. I usually press seams open, but as you can see from the picture, I let the seams dictate to me how they wanted to be pressed (fig. 5). With foundation piecing, since you're working with a mirror image, you are basically sewing upside down and backwards. Thus the reason for the full-sized drawing.

I starch *everything* so when Nancy sent back the center I had to restarch the whole thing again. It turns out more square. I also used three tubes of washable glue sticks as I flipped and sewed. I prefer the finest silk pins for pinning the segments together at the intersections because they are longer, thinner, and enable you to get the seams to match.

Because I wanted the teeth in the blue fish not to shadow, I doubled the white fabric—not a problem with weight because it was to be machine quilted. For the machine quilting, I marked with blue water-soluble markers for the fish heads and eyeballs. For the rest, I just freelanced it and hoped for the best.

I had a heart-attack moment five days before the quilt had to be at the museum. I spent three hours looking for the remaining dark blue that was to be the binding. I forgot I had used it in the outside border. I raced to my favorite fabric store *praying* I would find a batik similar in shade. I couldn't believe my luck in finding the same batik but then remembered Nancy saying one of the blues bled like crazy. Of course, this was that blue. I put it in hot water and watched the bleeding, totally freaking out. Where in the world is Retayne™ rinse when you need it? I remembered in dying fabric you used soda ash to set the dye. That I had, so I mixed up a small portion and the blue finally settled down. Don't you just love quilting?

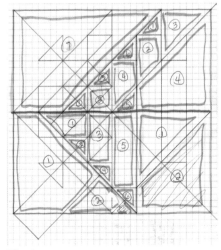

Fig. 4.

Fig. 5.

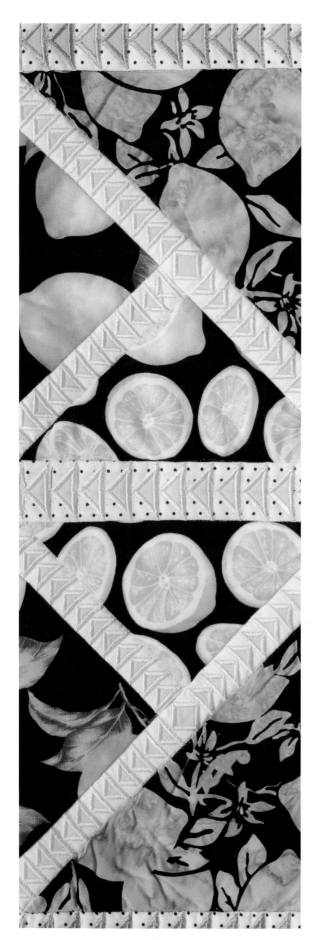

Nancy's photo by Nancy Lambert

Nancy Lambert
Pittsburgh, Pennsylvania

I started sewing when I was in grade school and continued to sew as a child and adult. My sewing hobby eventually turned to quilting and now I quilt almost every day. Some days I may just sketch an idea or look at a magazine.

I have always enjoyed making quilts and have tried a large variety of techniques and methods. While I have made many traditional pieced and appliqué quilts, most of my more recent quilts have tended to be modern interpretations and not traditional patterns. I gravitate towards clear and spring-like colors and I often find that lemon and lime appear in many of my quilts

Over the years, I also have tried to dye and paint fabrics to achieve a unique look. You can always learn something new by trying a new or different technique. Skills and techniques that are used from one project can carry over to a future project.

I enjoy both designing and making quilts. Often when I am busy I tend to sketch out ideas and then improve on the sketch. Many if not most of these ideas never make it into a quilt, but I enjoy working on the design. There are many similarities between traditional block and more modern art interpretations. The basic triangle that was used in this quilt is a widely used shape that makes up many quilt blocks and patterns.

Inspiration & Design

When I learned that the theme for the contest included triangles, I had an immediate idea to make a quilt entirely of triangular shapes. I started to sketch out various combinations of triangles. I divided triangles and played with arranging them. I eventually ended up with having gradations from large to small triangles. The basic block consisted of three triangles. If you take a square and divide it in half and then take one of the triangles and divide that in half you will end up with three triangles. This was the unit block that was then used throughout the quilt (fig.1, page 32).

Four-unit blocks were used at the center of the quilt. For the second border around the center, a series of unit blocks was used again, but this time, the original unit block was scaled down by one-half. Similarly the third border was a set of unit blocks, scaled down by one-quarter from the original center blocks.

LEMON-LIME 56" x 56"

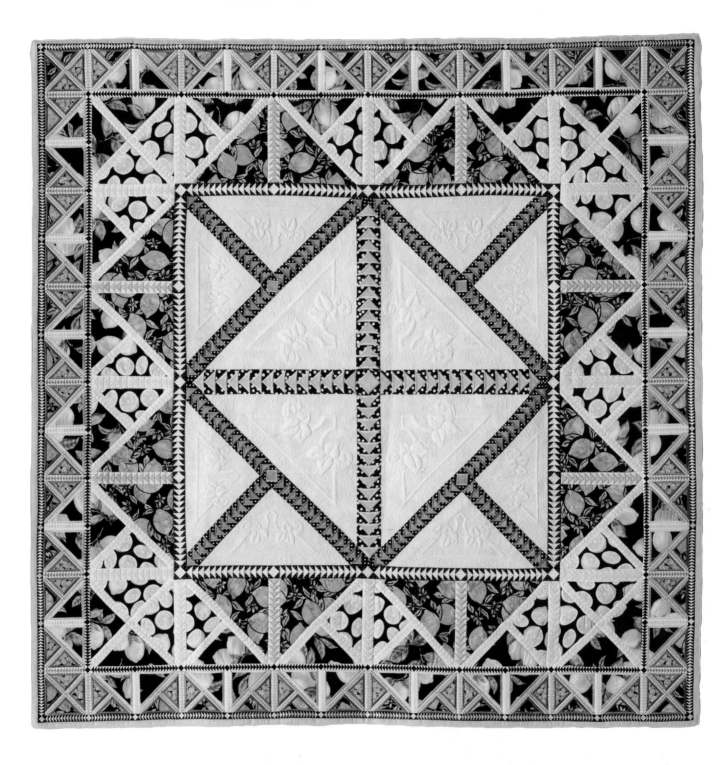

*I gravitate towards clear and spring like colors and I find
that lemon and lime appear in many of my quilts.*

After the triangular blocks were in place, I added a border around each triangle to give it more definition and interest. This border consisted of smaller triangles. When combined with the adjoining blocks, they make a Flying Geese pattern.

One of the difficulties of designing this border was that what you can sketch on paper is often difficult to actually piece or appliqué on a quilt. You can easily draw a small detail very accurately, but it took several attempts to find a way to put this idea into the quilt because some of the

Fig. 1.

Quilting motif by Helen Squire

Fig. 3.

Fig. 2.

triangles were less than a quarter-inch in size. I originally tried piecing the small triangles together. This worked well for the middle of the quilt, but proved very difficult for the outer triangles because their size was so small. I ended up machine appliquéing the triangles to the fabric base, preparing them by using a fusible web on the wrong side of the fabric.

Another complication arose trying to cut these smallest of triangles. I fused several layers of a lightweight interfacing to the triangle fabric base, fusing one layer at a time. Then I added the fusible web under the prepared base. The multiple layers of the interfacing gave the triangles enough body to handle them more easily and cut very small pieces. These layers of interfacing also had the added benefit of not allowing any shading to show through the triangles. Some of the triangles are light in color and the base they are placed on is very dark. Without this additional interfacing, the dark background would have showed through the light triangles.

Technique

My quilt was based on triangles, varying the sizes. The first is full size, then one-half size and one-quarter size. The full size can be any finished size that you'd like and then the other sizes are proportionate. These triangles can be copied and duplicated to create a variety of designs.

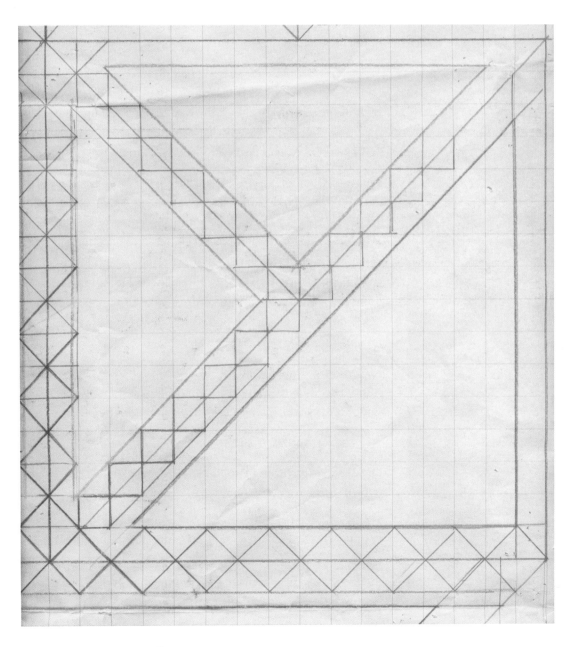

Finalist
Robin Brooks
Asheville, North Carolina

As far back as I can remember I have always loved fabric and all its endless possibilities for creativity. Growing up, my mother, Jewel, who is a talented seamstress, would look at an outfit at the local store and copy it to look even better. Most kids were ashamed of their clothing if it was handmade, but not me. I was proud to wear the clothes that she made for me. Those were special times, the hours spent in Mama's sewing room.

My grandmother, Etta, was the quilter in the family. I remember watching her cut a shape out of cereal box cardboard and glue a piece of sandpaper to the back for her template. She loved hand piecing with brightly colored fabrics and most of her quilts were scrappy. She said the bright fabrics made the quilt shine.

I come from a long line of quilters so it was only natural for me to follow in their footsteps. Using some of Mom's polyester fabric scraps, I made my first quilt in the early '70s. It was the traditional Grandmother's Flower Garden. The polyester was so heavy, hand quilting was impossible, so I tied it with cotton crochet thread. I still have that quilt and it will never wear out!

Quilting was not a part of my life for several years. Other things took priority but I knew some day I would return to this wonderful craft. In 1996, my best friend, Dennisa, and I decided to take a few classes. Well, needless to say I was hooked all over again. I continued to take a variety of classes and started buying patterns, books, and fabric for a fabric stash. Eventually I started taking traditional patterns and changing them to make them my own. I was introduced to Electric Quilt, a computer quilt design program, and I've never been the same. Now I am only limited by my imagination and it's really exciting.

Most of my quilts are high in contrast. I love for the pattern to really stand out and pop. Pattern design, proportion, and color selection are very important to me. In the past few years I have challenged myself to enter quilts in the local Asheville Quilt Guild Show. They have won a variety of ribbons, which inspires me to keep creating. I am also blessed to be a part of a wonderful group of quilters called the Wee Bees. Their friendship and encouragement is never-ending.

Having always been in awe of the artists of the Southern Highland Craft Guild, I've dreamed of being a member. Born and raised in western North Carolina, preserving my own and others' quilting heritage is important to me. So last year, I applied for membership and was accepted. I am very honored to be a part of this wonderful organization.

Robin's photo by Tim Barnwell

RADIANCE 65" x 52"

When I design a block on the computer, the first thing I check is whether it can be paper pieced.

Besides designing and making quilts, my husband, Larry, and I live on a small farm where we enjoy farm life, raising animals, and gardening.

We especially enjoy our colored angora goats, chickens, and French angora rabbits. My other hobbies include spinning, knitting, crocheting, and cooking.

Inspiration & Design

Inspiration for a quilt comes from many different places—antique quilts, traditional patterns, nature, and life's joys and troubles. All these things inspire me to create a quilt. The colors I choose usually reflect my mood and thoughts at the time.

I first discovered the MAQS New Quilts from an Old Favorite contest while attending the International Quilt Festival in Houston, Texas, a few years ago. It was fascinating to see how the artists had created amazing quilts from one traditional quilt block. I wished that one day I might have the confidence to enter such a challenging competition. A couple of years ago I started a quilt for the contest, but I was disappointed in the

finished piece so I did not enter it. This past year the Wee Bees decided to have a challenge called "My Personal Challenge." The first thing that came to my mind was the MAQS contest!

Technique

Paper piecing is my favorite method of piecing. When I began studying the Sawtooth block pattern, the first thing I thought about was whether it could be paper-pieced. With a quilt design computer program, I started deleting and drawing additional lines and manipulating other areas of the block (fig. 1).

Next, I wondered how to set the block. I chose a layout that is traditionally used for the Tumbling Blocks pattern (fig. 2).

Since this quilt is very geometric, I chose bright high contrast fabrics starting with reds and then added fabrics that complemented each other.

My favorite paper to use for paper piecing is vellum. It is more expensive but since it is slightly transparent it's easier to see sewing and placement lines. It is sturdy and available in both 8½" x 11" and 11" x 17" sizes.

RADIANCE is made up of seven sections. Each section was printed on several sheets of paper and taped together to form the paper-pieced patterns. The large oval disks were traced onto freezer paper, which was cut out and used as templates. The quilt was appliquéd to the background.

Fig. 1.

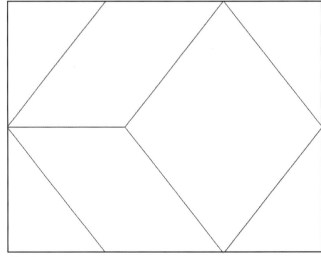

Fig. 2.

Working with one section at a time, I separated the paper-pieced patterns into smaller workable sizes, using a short stitch to make the foundation easier to remove (fig. 3). After finishing the paper piecing, I trimmed all the edges to a scant ¼", then turned under the trimmed edges using a glue pen. The glue pen, which can be found at most office supply stores, is much smaller in diameter than a glue stick, which makes for less waste and less mess.

To help with placing each section onto the background fabric, I made a see-through placement template by printing the section onto vellum. I could then lay this over the background fabric and position the pieces to be appliquéd underneath. Since the vellum is semi-transparent, I could move and adjust the pattern pieces as needed.

I appliquéd the finished pieces to the quilt background fabric, using invisible thread and a very tiny zigzag stitch. On the back side of the quilt top I cut away the background fabric over the paper-pieced patterns and gently pulled the paper out. Tweezers are helpful in the corners and a light spritzing of water will help loosen a stubborn piece of paper.

For me, choosing a quilting pattern is by far the hardest part of making a quilt, but it is very important. Soon after starting a quilt I am thinking of how I want to quilt it. I have even designed some quilts around a quilting pattern. Quilting adds dimension, texture, movement, and color to a quilt. Free-motion quilting is my favorite method for machine quilting, but I also enjoy straight or decorative stitches using a walking foot. Experimenting with different threads is always lots of fun and adds interest to a quilt.

I enjoy designing the quilt label on the computer. With any publishing software, a variety of shapes, fonts, borders, and graphics are right at your fingertips. When I am satisfied with the label, I print onto a Printed Treasures™ sheet. These fabric sheets are especially designed for inkjet printers. After printing, peel off the paper backing and you have a soft and pliable sheet of fabric with your label on it. All that's left is to sew it to the back of a quilt.

Fig. 3.

Finalist

Sherri Bain Driver

Tucson, Arizona

After living most of my life in Colorado, my husband and I moved to Tucson in 2005. We love the stark beauty of the desert. Our house backs up to an open area where we often see wildlife. Lizards are frequent visitors to our backyard where they find refuge under rocks and engage in crazy antics. When I have the time, I enjoy watching the animals.

I love to make quilts, but sometimes the idea of going into my sewing room to create "something" can be daunting. I have an enormous stash of beautiful fabrics and quilt designs spinning around in my head. I always have several quilts in various stages and could easily find two dozen UFOs around my house that I really do intend to finish some day. Sometimes I just don't know where to start. I need to narrow down the infinite choices. That is why I enjoy working within a framework or set of guidelines that the MAQS contest provides.

Quilting is about fabrics, color, and creativity, but most of all it's about the friends I've made along the way.

Inspiration & Design

Through the years, the MAQS contest has pushed my technical and design skills farther than I ever could have imagined. I generally start without a preconceived notion of what I want to make. I play with the design and fabric and prepare for an exciting quiltmaking journey. I'm constantly amazed at the different directions we quiltmakers take when challenged to make a quilt using the same traditional block.

Playing with two very different Sawtooth blocks, I created the center with one version and a setting with another. Of the Sawtooth blocks shown on the MAQS Web site, the version with triangles converging on an eight-pointed star seemed most interesting to me. I wondered what would happen if the groups of triangles spiraled into the star rather than taking a straight path. A quick sketch of that idea looked promising, so I continued drawing. Later, while flipping through my sketchbook, I found a previous doodle of a lizard decorated with geometric patterns. Now I had an idea I was excited about.

My fabric choices generally begin with a few multicolored ikat fabrics pinned to my design wall. Several weeks may pass as I add more fabrics, refine my quilt sketch, and assign fabrics to certain areas of the quilt. I continue to add and subtract fabrics until I have an interesting mix of colors that includes a dark and a light, and I have made enough decisions to begin the project. The fabrics in this quilt migrated toward each other in my sewing room—they just seemed like they needed to be together in a quilt.

Sherri's photo by Diane Graham

A Gathering of Geckos 54" x 54"

Although previously reluctant to do the A word, this contest took me on an unexpected appliqué adventure.

Technique

Before I start to sew a new quilt, especially one that incorporates techniques that are new to me, I try to anticipate problems that may arise. I had several concerns with making the center of this quilt, so I looked for solutions to the following questions:

What material could I use to foundation piece the geckos' bodies and also use as a firm base for turning and gluing the edges? Was there a product that could stay in the quilt? I read about Sharon Schamber's machine-appliqué technique, in which she used a leave-in stabilizer to make templates for appliqué patches. So I used a similar product, RinsAway™ water-soluble backing, for my foundation material and appliqué templates.

How could I stabilize the striped fabric that didn't have much body and would have bias edges? I wanted to use an iron-on paper product to stabilize it throughout the machine-appliqué process that could be torn away afterwards. Freezer paper would be too stiff to manipulate under the sewing machine. With the many turns required to appliqué the gecko feet and toes, the freezer paper would certainly crinkle, tear, and come loose from the fabric. Sulky® Totally Stable™ stabilizer solved the problem.

How could I mark the striped background to assure accurate placement of the geckos? Their toes and tails are close together, so I felt that accurate placement was critical to the success of the design. I traced guidelines and the positions of the gecko appliqué onto the stabilizer before it was ironed to the wrong side of the striped fabric.

My original sketch was drawn on graph paper with each square representing $2^{1}/_{2}$" (fig. 1). I used this tiny sketch to determine the sizes of all of the pieces in the quilt, rotary cutting some patches and making templates for others.

To make a full-size pattern, I taped freezer paper together to make a piece large enough for the center. Lines were drawn horizontally, vertically, and diagonally to divide the paper into eighths. I drew lines to indicate the outer edges of the center octagon and then drafted the center star. I drew one gecko with its nose between star points. Drawing freehand, it took many tries to get it right. Fortunately, freezer paper is sturdy enough to withstand lots of erasing.

For inspiration I had collected pictures and drawings of lizards torn from catalogs and magazines. I decided that three toes per foot were enough, even if not anatomically correct. When I was satisfied with the gecko, I traced it and any guidelines onto see-through template plastic and cut it out. I used this plastic cut-out to draw the remaining seven geckos on the large pattern, matching

Fig. 1.

Fig. 2. Enlarge to desired size.

guidelines on the template to the horizontal, vertical, and diagonal lines on the freezer paper for proper positioning (fig. 2).

To reinforce the striped fabric for the center, I taped together pieces of stabilizer, then traced the geckos, guidelines, and star onto the non-adhesive side. I carefully untaped the four sections of stabilizer and ironed them to the wrong side of the striped fabric. I cut out the stripe, adding several inches to the outer edges of the octagon in case the fabric shrank during the appliqué process. I sewed the striped sections together and added extra seams to the central star to make it more complex than a regular eight-pointed star, then set the star into the center of the striped section.

I adapted Sharon Shamber's appliqué method for my quilt and used RinsAway backing for foundation piecing the gecko bodies and templates for appliquéing the feet. The most challenging part of this quilt was making the gecko feet. Because the toes were so tiny, I had decided to limit each foot to three toes—but that's still 96 toes!

Some lizards are made with striped fabric, so I pieced the legs to make the stripes bend at the joints. When all the gecko parts were prepared, I placed the striped center over a light box to position the bodies and feet and appliquéd them using a narrow zigzag stitch and monofilament thread (fig. 3).

To make a gecko, trace all lines of the gecko pattern onto RinsAway backing. Foundation piece the gecko body, following numerical order and trimming excess fabric after each patch addition. Leave about $3/8$" turn-under allowance all around the outside edge of the body. Turn the edges to the wrong side of the foundation and glue with a water-soluble glue stick. Trace the legs onto the backing and cut them out. Glue them to the wrong side of the fabric and cut them out, adding about $3/8$" turn-under allowance all around. Carefully clip inside curves, turn the allowance to the back, and glue in place. Position the gecko legs and body on your background and appliqué in place.

Fig. 3.

Nancy's photo by Gerald Reuter

Nancy Eisenhauer
Belleville, Illinois

I have been sewing since I was a child. My mom showed me the basics on an old Kenmore and then let me experiment. I started with doll clothes and went on to garments. I sewed most of my clothes until I started teaching. Then for most of my career, I sewed very little. My first two quilts were tee-shirt quilts for my two children. I saw an article in a magazine that gave some good directions and thought I could do that. My sister-in-law, Gail, who was already a quilter, gave me some good tips and lots of encouragement. That was in 2001. I have since retired from teaching school and have become obsessed with quilting. I have no desire to go back to garment sewing. This is so much more fun!

I have always been attracted to bright colors and interesting textures. I am a fan of artists of the impressionistic period. I like the fact that they shunned the artistic styles of the day to create something new and exciting. Claude Monet's study of light and his determination to portray everyday things in such a beautiful style inspire me. I am also a fan of Vincent van Gogh. I love the textures and movement in his work. I admire Piet Mondrian for his geometric discipline and use of bright, simple color.

Much of my inspiration comes from art, particularly painting. Traveling also provides stimulation for new ways to express myself. My camera comes in handy to capture a pattern or scene of particular interest.

The smartest thing I did when I retired in 2006 was to join a quilt guild. The members of Hearts and Hands have been a source of knowledge, techniques, encouragement, and most of all, friendship. I have signed up for almost every workshop the guild has offered. I have learned something from each professional quilting teacher. Three of us from the guild have formed an art quilt group. Jacque and Pam are nothing less than spectacular mentors in the area of art quilts. They have convinced me that I can do more than I thought I could and have pushed me way out of my box.

In addition to quilting, I have started making altar cloths and banners for my church. There is a lot of joy in trying to create a visual representation of scripture or a special season or event. The first altar cloth I did was for Father's Day. It is made entirely from

I always considered teaching to be a creative endeavor.
Quilting has filled that void since I retired.

Fig. 1.

Fig. 2.

men's ties collected from the congregation. I have made cloths and banners for the summer growing season, fall harvest, Lent, and Advent. The set of which I'm most proud is the hangings I did for my daughter's wedding. I used the Double Wedding Ring block to make an altar cloth. For the banners I used pieced and paper-pieced blocks of Christian symbols as well as other symbols of new life. My next project for church is an altar cloth for Mother's Day. This time I'm collecting handkerchiefs, lace, and other things moms love.

Inspiration & Design

I am hardly a traditional quilter, but I love to play with the possibilities in old quilt blocks. I remember the quilts my grandmother made, usually one a year. She used traditional quilt patterns, appliquéd or pieced, and quilted by hand on her quilting frame in the front room. When I started quilting, I wanted to use some of those old blocks, but in a new way. Before I even knew about the New Quilts from an Old Favorite contest, I used the Monkey Wrench block to recreate van Gogh's *Starry Night*. When I saw an ad for the contest in the Summer 2007 edition of *American Quilter*, I knew I had to give it a try. This year's block, Sawtooth, was particularly appealing to me. I love geometry and manipulating shapes.

As I continued to page through the magazine, an article by Lura Schwarz Smith, "Traditionals Transformed: New Twists on Old Favorites," caught my eye. She uses straight-line and curved-line distortions of traditional blocks to make them fit particular elements in her pictorial quilts. I could almost feel the gears turning in my brain.

I knew the quilt was going to be circular in design. I made a couple of freehand drawings starting with a LeMoyne Star in the middle with triangles spiraling out from the center. It looked like Flying Geese that were going in every direction. I looked at that a few days and decided that wasn't what I wanted. I started again with the star in the center, but this time I used something that looked more like a Sawtooth block to fill the spirals. I liked that much better.

When I designed this quilt, I had just taken a two-day workshop with Jane A. Sassaman in which she taught us to use our "internal compass" to make graceful, natural arcs. I began with concentric circles and divided the design into eight pie-shaped pieces. Then I used Jane's method to make a pleasing arc to outline each section and filled in the

Sawtooth elements. I knew I wanted the quilt to be done in gradations of colors. I started shopping for fabric and it took more than one shop to find what I needed. I cut small bits of the fabrics and glued them to the drawing to make sure I was going to like what I had chosen (fig. 1).

As you can see from the photo, the outer arc changed from the mock-up to the final quilt (fig. 2). I thought the mock-up looked too much like a flower and I wanted it to resemble a circular saw blade. I had already decided that I would call the quilt CIRCULAR SAW in honor of my father and his love of saws (or any other tool, for that matter).

As I started to work on the quilt, the center became a problem. I pieced a LeMoyne Star in two shades of yellow. It didn't work for the center at all. I had no idea what to put there, so I began to work on the spirals instead, leaving out the center part. As it turned out, I finished all the spirals and sewed them together before I solved the center problem.

Technique

Many of Jane Sassaman's designs are free form, so she fuses all her fabric to interfacing to control the bias and give her fabric more stability. I had just used this technique in her workshop and I liked it, so I decided to use it on CIRCULAR SAW. For the large background sections, I traced the pattern on the fusible, cut it out on the line, and ironed the fusible to the fabric. When I cut out the fabric, I added the $1/4$" seam allowance. By doing this, I kept the bulk to a minimum when piecing the large sections together. For the triangles, I fused the fabric first, and then traced the triangle sections onto the fabric and cut them out on the lines.

I carefully placed the triangles on their appropriate sections, making sure they were aligned as I wanted. I used a loose satin stitch around all the raw edges of the shapes to appliqué them to the background. As I finished all the sections in one spiral, I machine appliquéd one section to the next. I constantly checked to make sure the sections would lie flat after they were sewn together. As I finished the spirals, I laid them on the full-size drawing I had made to confirm their fit.

Now that I was finished with the spiral sections, the most challenging part of the project began. I decided to machine appliqué each spiral to its neighbor. I pressed

under the seam allowance on the convex side of each section. Then I carefully positioned it on the concave side of its neighbor, again aligning it to match my full-scale drawing and pinning it. After sewing each seam, I again checked to make sure the quilt was still flat.

Once all the spirals were together, I had no choice but to address the center. A friend had suggested that I continue the spiral all the way to the center. There is a lot to be said for letting a project sit for a while until it tells you what it needs. I finally figured out what I wanted (or what it was telling me!) and started playing with some of the leftover scraps. The spiral to the center was the answer! It turned out to be my favorite part of the quilt (fig. 3).

Now the problem was how to attach the center, since the area around the center was already in place. Reverse appliqué was my solution. I appliquéd the black background to the center of the quilt top and then applied the remaining triangles to the black fabric. I cut, fit, and appliquéd the black background around the finished design.

Again the top sat as I figured out how to quilt this design. Simplicity won out. I simply followed the lines of the design to accent the design, not compete with it. I used an ornamental overlapping triangle stitch to quilt the background in an echo fashion. I had been determined to heavily quilt this piece, but then good common sense and my sister-in-law prevailed.

Fig. 3.

Robin's photo by Jane Mueller

Finalist
Robin Gausebeck
Rockford, Illinois

I like to call myself an accidental quilter, even though I have known how to sew since middle school. About four-and-a-half years ago, my husband and I finally decided to do something with a tall wall in our stairwell that just cried out for something dramatic. I figured a length of interesting fabric would be just the thing, so we headed out to a new fabric store to see what we could find. I came across a book of quilts that looked easy to do and incorporated oriental-themed fabrics that appealed to us both.

I knew absolutely nothing about quilting. I didn't even have a decent sewing machine, but I enlarged one of the designs so it would be about eight feet long and went at it. The result was what one could have expected—it is really striking to look at but the workmanship is terrible.

The process of buying fabric and working with color brought out some latent creativity that I never really knew was there. I was hooked and quilting has become my passion (some might say obsession). Quilting has changed the way I look at the world around me, enabling me to see colors and patterns in new ways. Everything I see has the potential to become a quilt. My design notebook is filled with ideas that I hope someday to transform into a work of art.

My quilts generally evolve backwards. A title pops into my head and then my job is to give that title life through my fabric. I have no art training, so this is usually the most difficult part of the process. All of my quilts, with the exception of the first one, have been original designs and I almost always tackle techniques that are beyond my skill level. I find that I have learned from the challenges that I present to myself and my quilts are more interesting because of that. I favor contemporary and art quilts that are playful and saturated with color.

My husband, Steve, is more than supportive of this passion of mine. He advises on color and design, enjoys fabric shopping with me (up to a point), and that very first year of quilting, surprised me on my birthday with a trip to the AQS Quilt Expo in Nashville. Last year, it was his idea to build an addition onto our home that would serve as a quilting studio for me. It is light, airy, and has plenty of room for storage and design and construction space. I feel inspired each and every time I walk into the room and feel privileged to have a quilting space to call my own.

I am lucky enough to have retired early from a career in finance. That freed me to explore what I wanted to do with the rest of my life. My guild has been a great source of camaraderie and encouragement and I have tried to take advantage of nearly every workshop that it organizes.

DOWN THE RABBIT HOLE...OR THE CHESHIRE CAT'S REVENGE 56" x 57"

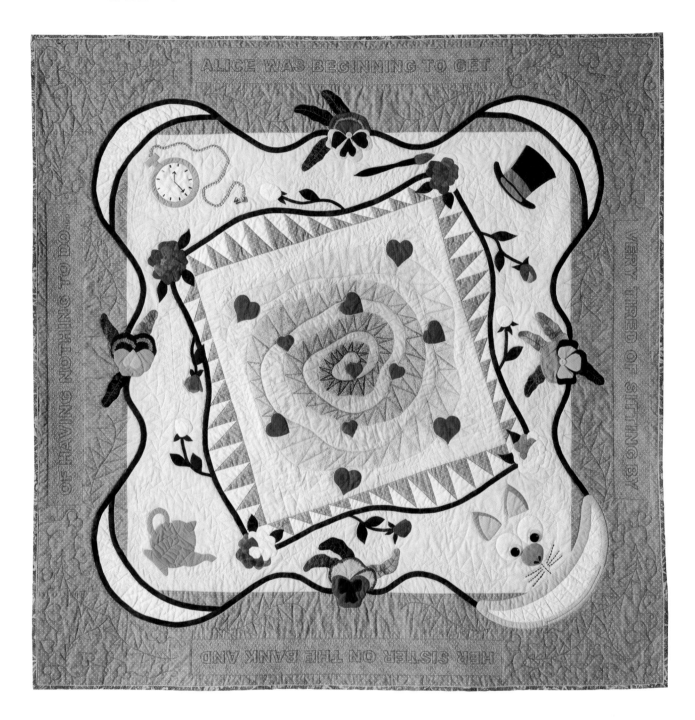

There isn't any activity in my life right now that brings me quite the same degree of pleasure and wonder that my quilting does.

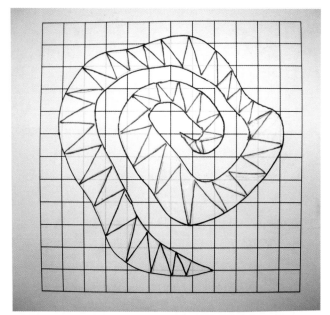

Fig. 1.

Fig. 2.

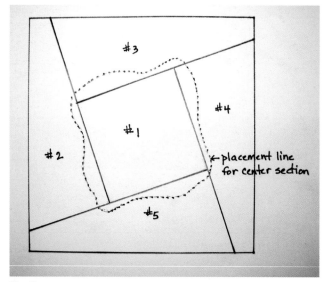

Fig. 3.

Mainly, I quilt for myself. I am not overly concerned with whether anyone else likes what I do, as long as I feel that I have succeeded in making art that pleases me. Winning awards always comes as a nice surprise but it doesn't drive my work.

Our four children are starting to marry and each one will receive a bed quilt from me as a wedding present. I still haven't quite mastered the art of quilting something gigantic on my machine, but where would the fun be if I only did things I already knew how to do?

Inspiration & Design

This was not the quilt I intended to make for this year's contest. I had designed a very striking quilt that incorporated Navajo motifs and the colors of the Southwest and I had even begun to pull fabrics from my stash. My husband, however, was not crazy about either the design or the colors and encouraged me to find some other way of expressing the Sawtooth pattern.

A two-day workshop with Libby Lehman really excited me about thread painting and I started to play around with some different shapes. The spiral idea just came to me and as soon as it did, the title invaded my brain and gave shape to the rest of the quilt.

As a child of the 1950s and '60s, I was much more familiar with the Walt Disney version of *Alice in Wonderland* than Lewis Carroll's original work and it was the cartoon Alice that really informed the quilt. The most difficult part of the design process was finding a way to portray the Cheshire Cat so that it was recognizable but steered clear of any copyright infringement. The text around the perimeter is the first sentence of Lewis Carroll's book.

I did not design the entire quilt at the start. I only knew I wanted a color-gradated spiral, with sawteeth painted in with thread against a yellow background. The rest of the quilt evolved after that center section was complete. As often happens, I wound up challenging myself to use new techniques.

Techniques

If nothing else, this quilt is a testament to the many ways we quilters can use that very pedestrian of materials—freezer paper. It proved to be invaluable.

My first step was to make a 24" x 24" freezer-paper square with a 2" grid. This represented what the yellow center section would look like when finished. I played around with a variety of spiral shapes with the Sawtooth pattern drawn in, drafting the designs onto freezer paper (fig. 1).

In this way, I could audition the spirals to see how each would look against the grid and, once I found the one that pleased me most, I could mark placement lines on the grid. After the yellow center section was pieced together, it was an easy task to iron the freezer-paper spiral on by referring to the placement marks I had made on the freezer-paper grid. Using decorative rayon thread and a shortened stitch length, I stitched around the outline of the spiral and the sawteeth, through the freezer paper, peeling it off when complete.

The blue and white curved Sawtooth sections were also drafted on freezer paper, but rather than stitch through the freezer paper, as in traditional paper piecing, I folded the freezer paper along the design lines and stitched right next to the fold. First, I perforated the freezer paper for ease of folding by stitching without thread along each fold line. Next, I matched the first two pieces of fabric, in this case one white and one blue, right sides together. I folded the freezer paper along the first stitching line, pressed it in place on the back side of the correct fabric with the fold line ¹/₄" away from the edge, and stitched the fabrics together at the fold line. I finger pressed the seam toward the blue. I ironed the next segment of the freezer paper down onto the back side of this blue piece, folded the paper at the seam line, trimmed the excess to ¹/₄", then aligned the next white piece of fabric with the edge of the blue, again right sides together. I stitched along the fold. This process was repeated with each succeeding sawtooth along the freezer-paper template (fig. 2).

This technique helped stabilize the entire section during stitching and the freezer paper was easily peeled off when each section was complete.

After determining the placement angle I wanted for the center section, I drafted five large templates onto freezer paper (fig. 3).

I ironed the templates to my fabric, making sure that the straight-of-grain edges wound up at the outside edges of the quilt. Leaving the freezer paper attached to the light yellow fabric, I stitched the five pieces together. Once the seams were pressed and the entire piece squared up, I removed the freezer paper and pinned my center section to the light yellow, being careful to align the seams properly. Then I machine-basted the center section to the light yellow and hand appliquéd the dark green stems. Only then did I cut away the light yellow fabric from behind the center section. I ironed 3" wide strips of freezer paper over the bias seams in the light yellow fabric to stabilize them until I could complete each section of appliqué.

I drafted the various Alice motifs on freezer paper, ironed them to the wrong side of the fabric, cut them out, and pressed under the raw edges. The freezer paper was removed after the shapes were sewn together onto the background.

To stitch the letters in the border, I traced them onto a length of freezer paper and ironed it to the border in the proper position. Using a shortened stitch length, I stitched around the outline of each letter through both the freezer paper and the quilt sandwich. I removed the freezer paper and to emphasize the letters, I traced over the stitching with a permanent blue pen.

The appeal of freezer paper is in how easy it is to position and reposition, if necessary, and the absence of pins that might distort the stitching. I buy giant rolls of it from my local grocery store and am constantly looking for more ways that I can use this versatile and inexpensive material in the design and construction of my quilts.

Julia's photo by Amy Graber

Finalist
Julia Graber
Brooksville, Mississippi

I was born and raised in the beautiful Shenandoah Valley near Bridgewater, Virginia. Growing up with six sisters and one brother was an enriching experience. We lived at the junction of North River and Dry River where we enjoyed swimming, ice skating, canoeing, and exploring in the woods. We also learned how to work, milking a cow by hand, mowing grass, and cleaning house along with sewing, cooking, baking, and laundry.

Now that I'm married, Mississippi is home to me. Paul and I have five boys and one girl. We live on a farm raising hogs and growing corn, soybeans, and wheat. Paul also helps his brother run a trucking company hauling stone, wood chips, grain, and fertilizer.

I come from a family of sewers. My grandmother not only sewed her own clothes, but also made many quilts and comforters. That tradition was passed on to the next generation and now on to me. I have many aunts who enjoy piecing and quilting. My mother, on the other hand, hasn't always enjoyed quilting. As a teenager she made the remark that she thought quilting was a waste of time. She would rather do things and buy chenille bedspreads. Mother wrote, "My wise mother-in-law did not insist that I learn to quilt. She simply invited me to her quilting bees. I gladly helped with the dishes and tried doing odd jobs rather than show my inability to quilt. Finally I couldn't resist and with her patience and supervision she taught me to quilt. It's an art that I now treasure."

Sewing began for me when I was in the eighth grade and I made a dress from red and white $1/8''$ striped fabric. I remember how the fabric had a way of playing with your eyes, making them dart around, leaving jagged empty black things floating by. I think it drove the home economics teacher crazy until I got it finished!

I made a few tied comforters in my late teens and after I married I continued making a few utility quilts for friends, charity, and myself. It wasn't until the late 1990s that I learned to enjoy and appreciate art quilts. I really enjoy the traditional quilts, but I like a new twist or contemporary flavor to them and the MAQS contest provides just that.

INDIAN FIRE RING 59" x 59"

*The Sawtooth quilt block evoked fond memories of the
years my father owned and operated a sawmill.*

Fig. 1.

Fig. 2.

Fig. 3.

Inspiration & Design

The Sawtooth quilt block reminded me of the jingle "When I went to Arkansas, I saw a saw that would out-saw any saw I ever saw saw!"

I can still see my father's sawmill—the big round five-foot saw blade with curled teeth and Father pulling the levers to cut the logs. The hired man stood at the end of the track and operated a smaller circular cut-off saw. He cut the slab wood with bark into pieces that would fit into our wood-burning stove. Father used a wedge to widen the cutting edge of the teeth and used a file to sharpen them.

Fig. 4.

Fig. 5.

For INDIAN FIRE RING I purchased Electric Quilt® software and played with the design using different colors and settings. In my first research I could only find one Sawtooth block (fig. 1) that I found in Electric Quilt, *Marsha McCloskey's Block Party*, and in Cheryl A. Adam's book, *Off Center Patchwork*. So I did some designing with just this block for a while. Here are four examples that I came up with (fig. 2).

Later I added the Lady of the Lake block with the sawteeth around the edges and made all sorts of quilt designs. You can see the progression of my quilt in the order of the pictures (figs. 3–5).

I'm gradually getting more confident with machine quilting on my home sewing machine. I marked a sawtooth design for the quilt in the background and borders and then echoed those sawteeth a couple times. Then, to highlight the Sawtooth motifs, I quilted a tight-looking, long, free-motion, serpentine stitch around them. I filled in the background with stippling using a variety of thread colors and types to help add interest.

SAWTOOTH: New Quilts from an Old Favorite

Karen's photo by James Kriegsmann, Jr.

Finalist
Karen Griska
White Plains, New York

I have always loved color and design. Even as a little girl, I remember weaving countless potholders, arranging and rearranging tiny plastic flowers on my grandmother's earrings, and making patterns with rocks, string, buttons, and whatever I could find. During Connecticut winters I used to break long icicles off our porch and stick them into snow banks, pointy end up, and then drip food coloring on them. They sparkled like jewels in the sunlight! I also loved to draw, paint, knit, crochet, embroider, and sew. I have spent many perfect afternoons creating colorful designs that delight my heart.

My mother taught me how to sew clothes when I was ten years old and I figured out how to make a quilt when I was thirteen. It was a one-patch made with four-inch squares of fabric left over from my sewing projects. There was no particular rhyme or reason to the fabric arrangement. That hadn't occurred to me. I bound the edges with store-bought blanket binding. The two-inch wide binding is paper thin because I only covered the outer $5/8$" of my quilt top—the standard seam allowance for dressmaking!

Quiltmaking is my passion. I love the creative process of designing a quilt. That's why quilting remains fresh and exciting for me after forty years and over 200 quilts, all original designs. I work quickly and improvisationally. I design my quilts as I make them. My results are better when I trust in the creative process than they would be if I planned my quilt in advance. I love to take advantage of the serendipitous moments that occur during the design process. I am often astonished by the finished quilt! That was the case with SAWDUST.

Antique quilts are my favorite source of inspiration. I especially like to study the state quilt survey books that showcase everything from the most primitive

SAWDUST (1,633 PIECES) 53" x 53"

I'm glad that my mother gave me some needlework skills and then let me take it from there because it gave me ownership of my creative journey.

utility quilts to the most elegant Mariner's Compass masterpieces. I find inspiration for quilts everywhere: looking out the window of an airplane, or seeing an arrangement of oranges at the grocery store or a wall of post office boxes. Ironically, making a quilt is a valuable source of inspiration for future projects. Going for a walk, visiting a museum, listening to music, and baking all fill my creativity tank.

When I begin a quilt, the first step is to start making blocks. Step two is to view them on the design wall (simply a large piece of off-white flannel tacked to a wall). At that point, the process takes on a life of its own. I stay open to new ideas and use lots of fabrics so if I run out of one, it won't matter. A digital camera is helpful for recording arrangement ideas in case I decide I want to return to a previous idea.

In recent years I have become fascinated with the design possibilities of using selvages as a main design element in quilts. This has become an exciting addition to my more traditional quilting. You can see these surprisingly delightful quilts in my new book *Quilts from the Selvage Edge*, published by the American Quilter's Society. You can also visit www.SelvageQuilts.com for inspiration and easy instructions. You are invited to exhibit photos of your creations there.

Inspiration & Design

Sawdust was made in response to this contest. It's my second quilt to be named a New Quilts from an Old Favorite finalist. My objective was to create a quilt that was pointy and spinning, a literal interpretation of the Sawtooth theme.

To emphasize the pointy piecing, I chose a large number of high-contrasting dark and light fabrics from my collection of old-fashioned prints, stripes, polka dots, batiks, and novelty prints. Some fabrics that would never be compatible in a quilt with only six fabrics look wonderful together in a scrap quilt. I love to explore a quilt that contains a huge number of fabrics and discover the surprises that the quiltmaker has hidden among them. It takes a long time to really get to know a scrap quilt.

First, I made four Pineapple blocks, the perfect place to start when making a quilt that is pointy and spinning. I learned how to make Pineapple quilts from Loretta Smith's book, *Pineapple Quilt: A Piece of Cake*. I started making them years ago "by the book," but now I make these blocks by eye using one-inch wide strips. The narrow strips enable you to get a lot of Pineapple design into a small space.

The little yellow square in the center of the quilt resulted from customizing one side of each of the four Pineapple blocks and leaving off the two adjacent corners. I could never have made that up in advance! That could only have happened as I arranged and rearranged the blocks on my design wall. No wonder I work late into the night when I'm on a design roll.

I invented a method for making fan blocks years ago that is fast and easy. Used alone, in pairs, or in clusters of four as shown in this quilt, fans can be quite dazzling. They are pieced "by eye" using rectangular strips, not wedge shapes. Paper piecing would have the disadvantage of each fan being exactly the same and it would take more time. If you make string quilts, you will understand this method instantly. It is described in the next section.

Using only two high-contrasting fabrics for the fans makes them stand out from the busy quilt, establishing the boundaries of the center medallion. They also serve to gently anchor the color theme, yellow and dark red.

To make sure that there was enough contrast, I found it helpful to view this quilt in low light conditions. I live near New York City and even in the middle of the night, it never gets completely dark. The city is like a big nightlight. Viewing the quilt at night, I could only see dark vs. light, enabling me to improve the fabric choices without color getting in the way.

The use of a reducing glass was also helpful. It is the opposite of a magnifying glass, giving you a thumbnail view of your design. This tool helps you determine if your design is crisp. It also reveals any trouble spots that need reworking.

Technique

My favorite quilts are the ones that look complicated but are actually easy to make, and SAWDUST is a perfect example. There is no math required to make this quilt. The blocks are not made to any predetermined size. You may ask, "How do you know that they are going to fit? How many are you going to need?" The answer is that I don't know.

If my border is too short, I add on. If it is too long, I trim some of it off. It may be that a border uses 15 and ⅓ blocks. That's fine. You will see that happening in SAWDUST. You can read more about this way of thinking about quilt design in Gwen Marston's book *Liberated Quiltmaking*, published by AQS. She is my favorite quilt artist. When I see her quilts I can't wait to get back to work in my quilt studio.

Half-Square Triangle Blocks

To make a large quantity of half-square triangle blocks, try this simple method that produces eight at once.

Cut two squares the same size, one dark and one light. (Mine are 6" x 6". That produces 8 half-square triangle blocks that are 2½" square.)

Put right sides together, the light fabric on top. Draw an X as shown (fig. 1).

Stitch ¼" from both sides of the two lines as shown. Press.

Cut as shown (fig. 2). Press open.

Fig. 1.

Fig. 2.

Fig. 3.

Fig. 4.

Fan Blocks

Making fan blocks by eye is fun and will jazz up even a simple quilt.

Choose a square ruler the size you would like your finished fan to be.

Cut your dark and light strips any width you choose. To get started, I suggest you choose a 6" or 6½" ruler and cut your strips about 2" wide (fig. 3).

Cut your first strip about 9" long for the center, as shown. Cut another strip a little shorter than 9".

With right sides together, sew a seam starting with a ¼" seam allowance, gradually increasing to about a ½" seam allowance, as shown (fig. 4).

Trim the seam allowance to ¼" the length of the seam and press open (fig. 5).

Continue adding strips in the same way until the piece you have made is larger than half your ruler (fig. 6).

Fig. 5.

In the same way, add strips to the other side (fig. 7). Press.

Place the ruler on your block and trim (fig. 8).

Join four fan blocks to mke the block shown (fig. 9.).

It is not necessary or even desirable that all the blocks be exactly the same. Some variation will make the quilt more interesting.

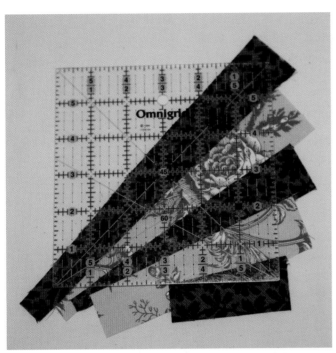

Fig. 6.

Fig. 8

Fig. 7.

Fig. 9

Robin's photo by Jon Haller

Finalist
Robin M. Haller
Carbondale, Illinois

Although my great-grandmother and my mother made quilts, I didn't become interested in quilting until we moved to a new city. My work at home as a back-of-the-book indexer was very solitary, so when a nearby quilt shop offered classes I signed up just to meet people.

After covering all the beds and making baby quilts for relatives, I became bored with the repetition of traditional blocks and settings and began to wander in another direction. The move to contemporary and art quilts came during a workshop on Double Wedding Ring as I struggled to make just five interlocking rings. (My son referred to it as the Olympics logo). I started strewing multicolored fabric spaghetti strands on top of a black background. That quilt is called COLORING OUTSIDE THE LINES.

There is not enough time in the day, in the year, in my lifetime, to draw all the pictures in my head. Inspiration comes from everywhere—a shadow on a wall, the juxtaposition of color and line, especially in nature, lines on a basket or a rug, the fractured image in beveled glass. In my Ideas file, I have a folder labeled Doorways and Ceilings, another marked Geometrics, another for Winter. There is one just for Boats, because I am intrigued by them, and one for Trees; another for Skies and Space. And there is a huge folder called Fantasy.

Making fiber art keeps me sane and makes me smile. In a personality survey for a medical study I was asked, "Given your choice, would you rather stay home or go out?" I fervently replied, "Oh, stay home!" The questioner looked at me anxiously and I knew I had given the wrong answer. I reassured him that staying home and working in my studio is a luxury and a refuge. The best days for me are those when I don't have to leave the house, but can take my coffee, go up to my studio, trailed by the three cats, and check the design wall, visible from the top of the stairs. That first look every morning inspires me to go on.

CONVERGENCE 51" x 63½"

Figuring out how to make one quilt at a time has required lots of trial and error, muttering under my breath, asking friendly critics to be brutally honest about my work, and then simplifying, simplifying, simplifying.

Inspiration & Design

Imagine tugging on a strip of Sawtooth points, and then whirling it about in ever-smaller circles. Now picture those points spinning off, flung out by centrifugal force and then drawn back in by an equal centripetal force until they converge.

This was what I saw inside my head as I was designing CONVERGENCE. A digital photo of the image in a triangle kaleidoscope of three overlapping circles was the basis of the composition (fig. 1).

Color inspiration came from a seed catalogue that I receive regularly. From every issue I tore out the page showing lime, periwinkle, and purple clematis—all three colors in one bloom. I put the clematis pictures up on the design wall, along with the kaleidoscope image, and contemplated turning them into a wall quilt.

Quilting is a medium, a way of producing the pictures I want to draw. Instead of dipping a brush in oil or watercolor, I thread a needle and paint. The sewing machine needle is my eleventh finger and with it I can produce magic. The fabric is my canvas, sometimes cut straight from the bolt, other times created by sewing strips together and cutting shapes from the new fabric.

On a sheet of newsprint the size of the finished quilt, I drew three overlapping circles to represent the clematis blooms. Somehow, in the freehand drawing process, my largest flower ended up with 11 petals instead of 10.

Drawing on paper-piecing techniques learned years ago, I pieced the petals by tracing over the original drawing, marking the tracing-paper template, and sewing from the back. A workshop taken with Ruth McDowell was very helpful in figuring out how to get the background sections around the petals to lie flat.

I have several more kaleidoscope images and the possibility of infinitely more, ready and waiting to be turned into new and very different quilts.

Fig. 1.

Fig. 2.

Technique

My art quilt group has accused me of making two quilts within the same quilt top. Sometimes I try to put an intricately pieced background behind an equally intricate, beautiful, but inappropriate foreground. Sometimes there are too many things going on in a small space. The remedy has been a learning process over the years that includes auditioning fabrics, adding or removing different design elements, or scrapping everything and starting from scratch. Doreen Speckman used to say, "Do you miss it when it's gone?" She was referring to the process of editing.

Sometimes a line drawing is enough to tell me I'm going the wrong way. For CONVERGENCE, whose working title was CLEMATISCOPE after the two photos it is based on, I made a colored drawing of three multicolored flowers (fig. 2). It was much too messy and unfocused and the petals were lost in the background. So I redrew each flower in one color. The full flower is green and the partial ones are blue and purple against a dark background in which green, blue, and purple Sawtooth triangles spin.

Fabric choice also helps in delineating the important elements of the quilt. In figure 3 the green petals are pieced and pinned in position on the master drawing. On the right are strip-sets of light fabrics that I thought would be the background between the petals, but it didn't look right. I ditched the strip-sets and settled on the mottled fabric that was already inside the petals. Again, the simplest turned out to be the best.

Those strip-sets are back in the stash, awaiting their day in the sun. After all, fabric doesn't go bad. Some of my favorite quilts have been constructed from leftover blocks and pieces from earlier works or from projects ripped apart and resewn into new and entirely original designs. UFOs that sulked in the corners of the closet for years have gained new life. They may have been edited out of one project, but they fit magically into a new one as if they were born there.

Fig. 3.

Yoshiko's photo by Takashi Kobayashi

Finalist
Yoshiko Kobayashi
Katano City, Osaka, Japan

I have enjoyed handicrafts and drawing ever since I can remember—knitting, embroidery, and making bags next to my mother while she made me dresses when I was a child. Mother and I both love fabrics. When I was about 30 years old, I made a big traveling bag in my own way to carry my sketchbook and water color box. I tore batting to pieces, spread it between two layers of cotton fabrics, and stitched on it by machine. I did not even know the word "quilting" in those days.

Ten years later I started making quilts after being inspired by a quilt exhibition in the late 1980s. Until attending a workshop with Nancy Crow in Osaka, all my quilts were hand pieced and hand quilted. But in those days, I was always troubled with a stiff shoulder. Now, I am wholly absorbed in quiltmaking on a machine.

I think that quiltmaking gives me the same delight as drawing. When my drawing hand is not so good, I know the fabrics will bring my quiltmaking to a new level. I enjoy every part of quiltmaking—the designing, choosing fabrics, and sewing. And I can find my own potential in the process of the work. I like that the repetition of thinking and trying refine the results for me.

I would like to continue quiltmaking in the future with something natural and close to my life, such as flowers, trees, birds, or landscapes.

Though I make non-traditional quilts, I very much like traditional patterns. They are attractive possibilities. Quiltmaking for the New Quilts from an Old Favorite contest is a new lesson for me every year. There are new exercises, new themes, and new techniques, bringing focus to quilting times in my daily life. All these things are a great pleasure for me. Also, I can meet other entrants' splendid quilts in the book.

Inspiration & Design

I usually switch on a video while I'm making a quilt so I can hear my favorite programs. I record dramas, movies, art programs, and more. They please me and are both relaxing and inspiring. I may even pick up a hint or advice for my daily life. Though it may be the reason why I don't make more quilts, it was during this time that I got a hint of an idea for my contest quilt.

While I was thinking about ideas for my quilt for the New Quilts from an Old Favorite contest, I was impressed with a scene in the old American movie *Wrestling Ernest Hemingway* with Robert Duval and Richard Harris.

HANA-BI (FLOWERS IN THE NIGHT SKY) 57½" x 75½"

A movie scene with fireworks going off in the distance inspired me to try to express the fire trail of hana-bi with a Sawtooth pattern.

The scene was that of two old men speaking while seeing distant *hana-bi,* "fireworks," on the horizon. The idea flashed across my mind that I might be able to express the fire trail of hana-bi with a Sawtooth pattern.

Hana-bi are common to Japanese since olden times. *Hana* means "flower." *Hi* means "fire," and when connected with *hana* it is pronounced as *bi* in Japanese. They say that the beginning of hana-bi was with the discovery of saltpeter in Old China around 500 B.C. In Japanese history, the first hana-bi were recorded about 200 years after that. In the Edo era, starting in 603 B.C., hana-bi became increasingly popular and continued to flourish. In the beginning of the Meiji era, in the late 1860s, the importation of coloring materials from abroad (potassium chlorate, strontium, barium,

etc.) allowed for making the most colorful and beautiful Japanese hana-bi.

Now in Japan, we frequently have hana-bi shows in various parts of the country every year, especially in summer. Shows have been held for various reasons such as contests, masses for the dead, dedications, festivals, or simply for enjoying the cool breeze. Traditionally hana-bi start with praying or dedicating a memorial service for the war dead, or victims of a flood, disaster, or big accident.

No matter how often, it is always a great pleasure to see hana-bi, hear their far-off sound, or to enjoy them on television during the summer. It is a great pleasure for children to hold sparklers in their little hands in the evenings of summer.

Fig. 1.

Fig. 2.

Technique

When selecting fabrics for the night sky of this quilt, I wavered between using black or navy. I decided on an indigo-dyed Yukata fabric that was given to me by my friend. Yukata is 100 percent cotton and used for making casual kimonos for the summer. I thought that it could represent the dimly-lighted space of the light trail.

I started by drawing a little sketch of my image in the sketchbook (fig. 1).

After scanning it, I enlarged it by four times, and printed it out (fig. 2).

I drew the actual sized plan, except for the middle hana-bi, on large gridded paper.

After transcribing each pattern on tracing paper, I cut them out and used them as templates to trace onto the fabrics.

The Sawtooth patterns of the hana-bi trail were pieced by the paper-foundation method. I transcribed the outline of the long light trails onto tracing paper, drew in all the piecing lines, and used the tracings as the foundation for piecing the fabrics.

After piecing the whole surface, I appliquéd and embroidered the yellow, blue, and green hana-bi using fused fabrics and organdy (fig. 3).

The machine quilting was done entirely by free-motion.

I adjusted and appliquéd little red organdy triangles for the red hana-bi in the upper part of the quilt.

For the middle hana-bi, I created a guideline of yarn to indicate the appliqué positions on the quilt. Then I adjusted and pinned the little silver organdy triangles alongside the yarn. I appliquéd them with an irregular zigzag stitch, then added embroidery and more quilting (fig. 4).

Fig. 3.

Fig. 4.

Barbara's photo by Erica Bartel

Finalist
Barbara Ortiz
Chester, California

Somehow, I always knew I would get into quilting. As a young child, I was envious of a friend who had a quilt her grandmother made with remnants of dresses she had sewn. No one in my family was a quilter, but the seed was planted. One day I would make a quilt.

I began sewing as a child and continued into adulthood, making clothes for my family. After marriage and three children, I went to school for a teaching degree and taught elementary school for 28 years. My interests have always included crafts and art. As an art major, painting became my passion with quilting lurking in the shadows of my mind.

About 30 years ago, a quilt shop opened nearby and I was on my way. My first quilt classes were taught by a wonderful quilter, Mary Brewer, who started us with pattern drafting and template making. From there we used our own templates, cut out patches with scissors, pieced and quilted our quilts by hand. I will always be indebted to Mary for this basic introduction.

Little did I know then that quilting would consume my time as well as the space in my home. When my children went off to college, their rooms became quilting rooms. My quilt library and fabric stash never seemed to shrink. They only grew.

After retiring from teaching, I became engulfed by the activities of a quilt guild, attending quilt shows, teaching quilting, quilt history, and working part time in a quilt shop. The owner, Ann Webster, inspired me to develop a beginning quilt pattern and a series of redwork patterns. Her encouragement gave me confidence and enabled me to broaden my quilting experience.

After sixty years we moved to a small mountain community, so there is more time for quilting. I spend considerable time drafting patterns, trying new things and studying quilts.

SILENT MOUNTAIN 52½" x 55½"

I like trying various techniques and early in the process of
making a quilt, I work to put my own touch on it.

Quilting has not only been a creative outlet but also a wonderful way to meet nice people and share a common interest. There is always something new on the horizon to keep us growing, and I am in awe of women's creativity shown through their exciting quilts.

Inspiration & Design

My inspiration was purely a desire to enter this contest. While exploring another pattern, I checked into the MAQS Web site (www. quiltmuseum.org). There I saw the Sawtooth contest and was drawn in. But it was August and I did not know how I could finish by November. It was all I thought about as a design began to take form. The mountain kept popping up in my drawings. My greatest challenge was the lack of time. Each day the deadline screamed at me.

The background fabric was another challenge. I had a piece of purple batik I wanted to use and other batiks just fell into place . . . until I got to the background. Nothing seemed to work. A quilt shop run did not produce the right thing and I was quite frustrated to think I might have to give up.

I continued making the mountain portion of the quilt, hoping something would turn up. Finally, after many searches in shops, I found the perfect hand-dyed sateen in my stash! But there was not enough. More frustration and searching until at last I found another piece of hand-dyed sateen of a complementary color that I had purchased several years before at a quilt show from the fabric dyer Wendy Richardson. I barely had enough, but the two fabrics worked when combined.

Originally, I had intended to add a border and a moon in the sky. The moon did not add anything to the quilt, there was not enough of the sateen for a border, and the other fabrics just did not work. This is the part of quiltmaking I like—when the quilt dictates the next step.

The most exciting time was when I showed it to a friend who asked me if I'd seen it from a distance. I had not, as I had been up close to it for so long. I was amazed at the depth and wish I could say I planned it that way. That is one of the wonderful things about what the right fabric can do.

This quilt was not only a challenge but also a learning experience in problem solving, researching vintage patterns, and an emotional

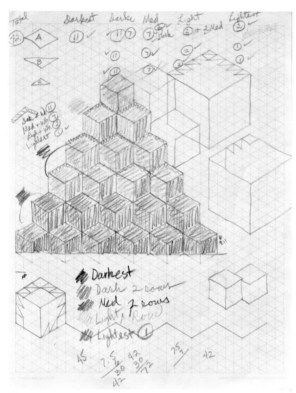

Fig. 1.

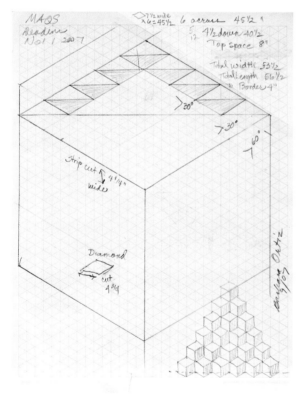

Fig. 2.

experience. I was excited and nervous to begin, frustrated over designs and fabrics, exhausted from taking on too much, anxious with anticipation after sending my entry, and full of delight to learn my quilt had been accepted as a finalist. The high point for me has come from other people being excited for me. My thanks to MAQS for offering this challenge each year.

Technique

I began with my drawing, first drawing rough sketches on a large piece of paper and then transferring the final one to graph paper (fig. 1).

Tumbling Blocks fit easily into my design. I was not looking forward to all those Y-seams, but it was good practice for me (fig. 2).

For the white snowcaps, I drew a foundation and paper-pieced them. The blocks were made by rotary cutting strips into 60-degree segments (fig. 3).

The background was not planned on paper as I was not sure how I wanted to do it. I thought I might appliqué the mountain onto a background, but when it came time I did not want to appliqué the Sawtooth portion with so many Y-seams. Time was running out when the idea of the extending strips arose. The background strips were cut in the same manner as the blocks and treated as an extension to each side block, meeting in the center at the top of the quilt.

After that, it was a matter of adding the batting, quilting, and binding. Simple quilting in the ditch and a bit of a zigzag quilting emphasized the mountain.

In preparation for this contest, I searched all my books for blocks with Sawtooth in their name. I drafted them and made each one, some traditionally pieced and some foundation pieced (fig. 4). They now appear on the back of SILENT MOUNTAIN.

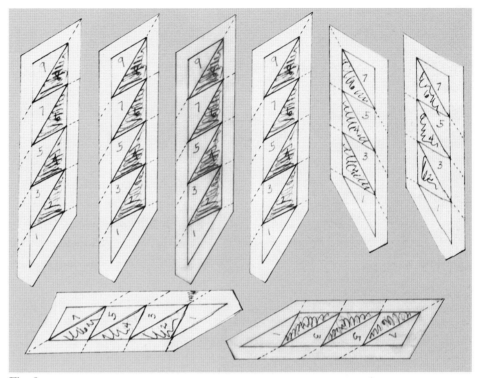

Fig. 3.

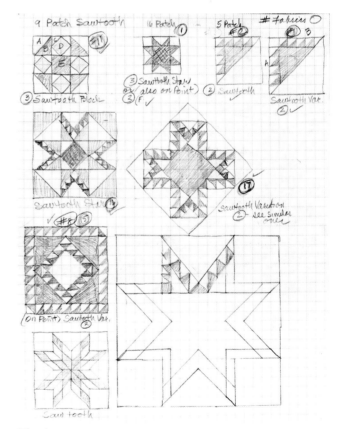

Fig. 4.

Helen's photo by Yuen Lui Studio, Inc.

Finalist
Helen Remick
Seattle, Washington

SPINNING OUT SPINNING IN 5 is my third entry in the New Quilts from an Old Favorite contest. I enjoy designing around a traditional block, taking it to new places while still paying tribute to quilts of the past.

I am now completing my second year of retirement, a major life transition not to be taken lightly, but one with many rewards. My daily rhythms are increasingly of my own making, and I feel less compelled to fill every moment with activity. In the transition from work to retirement, quilting was at first a substitute for work. I am now working on putting quilting in a more relaxed place so that it does not have to be front and center at all times. This change is giving me time to learn new skills instead of focusing primarily on production.

While I had used computers in my work, my focus had been more on data manipulation and writing. For this quilt, I finally opened the Adobe® Illustrator® software I had bought several years ago and took on learning a new program, different from anything I had previously used. I now incorporate the computer into aspects of my quilt design process.

Quilting is in the midst of rapid change, in both design and technical terms. Art quilts are expanding the notion of what a quilt is, and the aesthetics of art quilts are making their way into traditional and innovative quilts. At the same time, the techniques are expanding, most notably in machine quilting and photo printing. I am trying out some of the new techniques to see which ones fit me and which ones do not, which ones are enjoyable and which are not.

Some technical aspects, especially machine quilting, have become so involved that quilt production is now often done by a team rather than by an individual. Like other quilters who enter shows, I must soon decide whether I can bring my skills up to the new standards or whether I can find someone with whom to develop an artistic partnership. I see that the machine-quilting techniques are driving design as well, much as the introduction of paper piecing did a few years ago. Ink-jet printing is just a few years behind in its influence, as the inks have improved. Where will I take my work next?

Inspiration & Design

With each new quilt, I try to add skills and push my limits, often while building on past interests. For this quilt, I wanted to learn to print on fabrics and to use computer programs in design, integrating these elements rather than making them the focus.

SPINNING OUT SPINNING IN 5 64" x 66"

Handwork is my favorite part of quiltmaking. It is quiet and contemplative.

This quilt represents the fifth in a series using a computer program written by Ned May, a Virginia artist. The program generates Fibonacci spirals such as the one I used for the central motif. Ned calls his program the "Custom Fibonacci Spiral Generator." The program allows the user to input a design from which it creates a spiral with a variable number of "arms." I have previously used a triangle as the design; for this quilt, I entered the more complex Sawtooth block. The quilt block was then rendered in a series of "squares" with curved edges and of varying sizes. The more complex basic block produced many piecing challenges, especially where many seams came together in one point.

As I machine quilted, I became aware of two things. When we hand quilt, without even thinking about it we adjust the tension of our stitch to correspond to the numbers of layers of fabric we are quilting at any given point; and machine quilters favor appliqué techniques and simple piecing designs in part because machine quilting is less forgiving than hand quilting. (It is also the case that increased surface design shows off better with simpler piecing.)

I like varying value in my quilts. Fabrics by RaNae Merrill and Caryl Bryer Fallert allowed me to explore the full range of values in the complementary colors I chose for the quilt. In two places on the quilt I supplemented commercial fabrics with ink-jet printing. As the quilt pattern became smaller in the middle of the quilt, I printed the pattern onto the darker value of the commercial fabric. In the chartreuse diamonds, I replicated the center motif. I expect that I will use printing in future quilts, likely more as a means of creating specific effects than as the main focus.

While I create a rough sketch of the total quilt before I begin creating patterns, I find that I am still making changes up to the last minute. The fabric version of the design may or may not look as I had first envisioned it. A "brilliant" idea or choice of fabric may or may not look as I had hoped it would. I enjoy this fluidity in the process.

As much as I love handwork, some design elements are best done by other techniques. Arthritis prevents me from hand quilting any longer. I find that I am adding surface elements as a means of increasing the amount of handwork. On this quilt, I couched perle cotton on the edges of the rays in the central motif and I embroidered around the printed designs

on the chartreuse diamonds. I suspect that I am about to take on a major appliqué project just as an excuse to do handwork. While hand appliqué is not in fashion at the moment and is certainly slower than machine appliqué, it does bring me much greater satisfaction.

Technique

I used a complicated means of translating a computer-produced design into a quilt. The program that generates the spiral can take data in only a limited format. I drew the original pattern using Adobe® Illustrator® software (fig. 1).

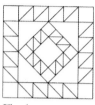

Fig. 1.

I scanned the image to produce an image meeting the format and size requirements of the spiral program. I input the resulting image into the program, setting parameters such as number of rays, and an $8\frac{1}{2}$" by 11" image was produced (fig. 2).

Fig. 2.

I chose which portion of the image I wished to use, enlarged it, and used the tile function in the print mode to print $8\frac{1}{2}$" x 11" pages to be glued together to create a master pattern for piecing. Where necessary I drafted the design beyond the original image. The master pattern was traced to produce the patterns for paper piecing the Sawtooth "squares" of the various sizes. In order to create the value gradation to the center, fabric for the squares was fussy cut with a range of values according to the distance squares were from the center.

The printed portions required many steps. In order to manipulate this image in Illustrator, I scanned it into a compatible format, enlarged the image, and traced portions of it by hand to create an Illustrator document. I determined which parts of the design I wanted to be printed in black and carefully outlined them separately so that they could be colored. Figures 3 and 4 show the resulting patterns for the green (fig. 3) and for the fuchsia (fig. 4).

Note that what is black on the green ray is fuchsia on the fuchsia ray, and what is black on the fuchsia ray is green on the other. After assuring that they were sized appropriately to fit with the enlarged master pattern, these patterns were used to print the central design.

To create the designs printed on the chartreuse diamonds, alternating green and fuchsia rays were reassembled to form a star (fig. 5).

The success of this step depended on the earlier careful drafting of the individual rays. This star and two of the rays, one from the green design and one from the fuchsia design, were resized to fit the diamond-shaped piece. I printed the fabric using an Epson® Stylus® Photo R1800 printer and DURABrite Ultra® pigment ink. The fabric was ironed to freezer paper and printed before being cut to size.

Fig. 3.

Fig. 4.

Fig. 5.

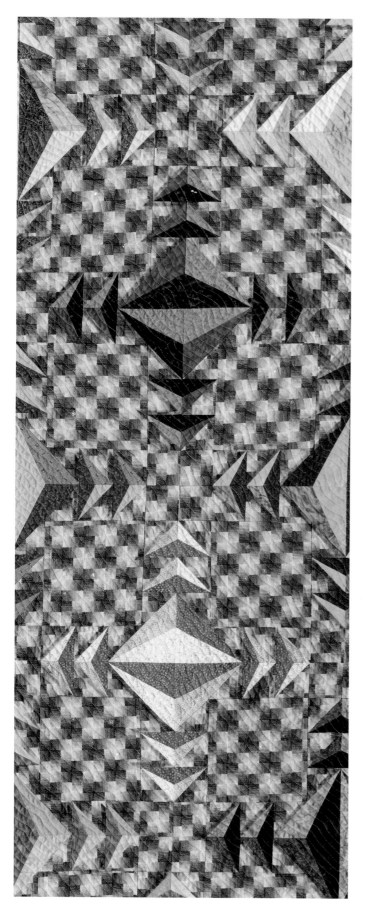

Cathy's photo by Angela Collier/Glamour Shots

Finalist
Cathy
Pilcher
Sperry

West Chester, Ohio

I have always had an interest in color and design, textiles, and clothing construction. This led me to Oregon State University where I obtained a degree in home economics education. Prior to starting my family, I taught home economics for eight years in both Oregon and Texas. My husband Dave and I, along with our two children, have moved back and forth across the country numerous times with his career. It was following a move in 1985 to New Jersey that my path crossed with that of a quilter and my life has not been the same since.

It was fun to take the clothing construction skills and techniques that I had perfected over the years and use them in this new arena. Not only was quilting a wonderful and creative outlet, I soon realized that quilting was the avenue to special friendships and a solid support system.

My mother taught me to sew when I was quite young and I brought my own daughter into the fold when she was six years old. I taught her how to use color, value, and contrast as well as all the technical skills of sewing. We spent many hours together shopping to replenish our stash and soon she had her own stash. Together we searched for new ideas and inspiration. Technique and design classes also made their way onto our calendars.

Little did I know at the time, but I was laying the foundation for future communication. When she reached high school and started looking at me as if I were the enemy, I realized that no matter how angry she might be with me, she would still "talk quilts." So many life lessons and conversations were intertwined with talk of color, design, and technique and with trips to quilt shops.

With a close friend who lives in Michigan, I recently started a cyber art quilt group. We e-mail a weekly report, which includes photographs of what we are

OUTBURSTS OF JOY 71½" x 71½"

*Quilting became my lifeline in more ways than one. To me it is spiritual
and represents family, friendship, fellowship, and more.*

working on. We include inspiration, techniques, frustrations, and revelations. This has been a tremendous source of encouragement and inspiration and has made us more accountable for our time and the creative process. One of the outcomes of this has been the "journal" that we now have to refer back to.

Like so many of our generation, Dave and I are now empty nesters. Our daughter is a high school geography teacher in Texas, and our son is a senior in mechanical engineering in California. So that we could put down more permanent roots, my husband left the corporate world two years ago to open his own business in the Cincinnati area. I am now working with him and my accurate quilting skills have been put to use in the large format digital imaging business. I do mounting, trimming, stitching, and finishing on many jobs including trade show banners and signage, vehicle graphics and wraps, as well as digitally reproducing and printing my quilts on canvas (www.speedprocinci.com).

This new career has seriously cut into my quilting productivity so when I do get a block of time, however small, I protect it for a session in my studio. I have started working on a smaller scale, which suits the time I now have. I do not spend a lot of time shopping any more, but instead use what I have on hand. I have discovered that I am forced to be much more creative and have come up with solutions I never would have found otherwise.

Inspiration & Design

OUTBURSTS OF JOY was designed when I was in Palm Springs caring for my mother-in-law following her open-heart surgery. I had a small pad of graph paper on which I drew a basic Sawtooth block in $^1/_4$ scale (fig. 1).

I photocopied the block to get multiple copies to play with. I laid these out on a piece of paper, turning the blocks until a design started to emerge. I then began bisecting all the triangles so there were three areas to shade in each large triangular shape to give dimension to the new design.

This was all done in pencil. It takes four Sawtooth blocks to create each design unit. The block has to be altered a bit as it goes around the outside edge so that the design has some resolution.

Fig. 1.

Fig. 2.

I refined and photocopied the finished design and used colored pencils to plan out the color placement (fig. 2).

One of the biggest challenges in making this quilt was that so many seams came together at the points. It became an issue of pressing and I finally had to ignore my old rule about pressing toward the darkest color. I pressed in the direction where I could reduce the greatest amount of bulk and created as many opposing seams as possible. I also pressed into a thick terry towel so that the seams had somewhere to go. It made the surface of the blocks much smoother.

The blocks were cut, sewn, and pressed one at a time. I kept the adjoining block on my ironing pad for quick reference as to which direction seams should be pressed. Some of the really bulky center seams were pressed open. As I finished using the reference block, it went up on the design wall and the newly finished block became the reference block. This became a system for keeping the construction of the quilt top organized and reduced mistakes.

Technique

Accuracy is a skill that I learned in clothing construction and it is probably the most important one that carried over into quiltmaking. OUTBURSTS OF JOY was made with templates. It was critical that the templates be drafted accurately and then tested before cutting all the fabrics. I always test my templates first, including pressing of each unit. Each unit is then measured for accuracy. If there is a discrepancy, it is corrected before being joined to the next piece. This is a square design that was kept square by pressing all the pieces on a gridded flannel surface. I used a stiletto to hold the small points and corners while pressing. Steam was used and the pieces were allowed to dry before being moved. I use a 60/8 Microtex needle, very fine thread, and a single-hole throat plate when accuracy is important.

I diagrammed each block and labeled the color, value, and templates. Each piece of fabric was laid into position before stitching to double-check the value placement (fig. 3).

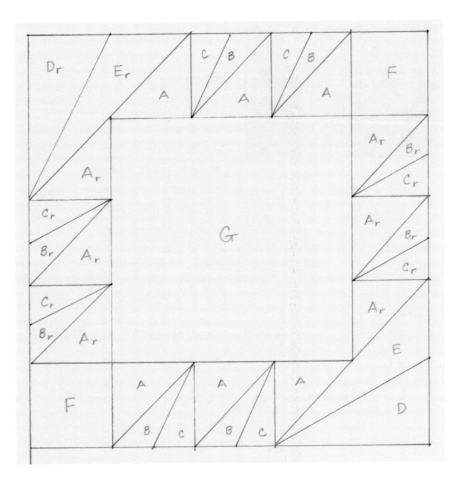

Fig. 3.

Fig. 4

Fig. 5

When I am in the beginning stages of piecing, I put finished units on my design wall to photograph. I print this out in black and white to make sure that I am achieving the dimension and/or movement I want. If it works in black and white, I can be fairly confident that the design is successful and I continue on (fig. 4).

After I stretch and pin my quilt for machine quilting, I stabilize the shape by quilting in the ditch with monofilament thread along all the major seam lines, removing the pins as I go. I only leave pins around the edges. I quilt on a Bernina® sewing machine and use small pieces of shelf-liner grip between my quilt and my thumb and index finger on both hands. This allows me to have control over the movement in my free-motion quilting.

When the quilting is finished, I block my quilt by pinning it to a carpeted floor, using a square to make sure it is lying straight. I use cool water in a spray bottle and spritz the entire quilt. It usually takes a couple days to dry. Then I give it a light steaming on my pressing board to make sure it is square.

When OUTBURSTS OF JOY was finished, the design did not float over the surface as much as I had envisioned. To create this extra layer, I painted shadows with a black Shiva® Artist's Paintstik® oil color. I made a stencil from template plastic and a color copy of one of the areas of the actual quilt and practiced on this before applying the paint to the quilt (fig. 5).

I love to add embellishments as a finishing touch. The background of this quilt was busy, but I wanted something on the surface to catch the light and add a bit of sparkle. The solution was clear sequins sewn on with clear faceted beads. They are unnoticeable unless they catch the light just right.

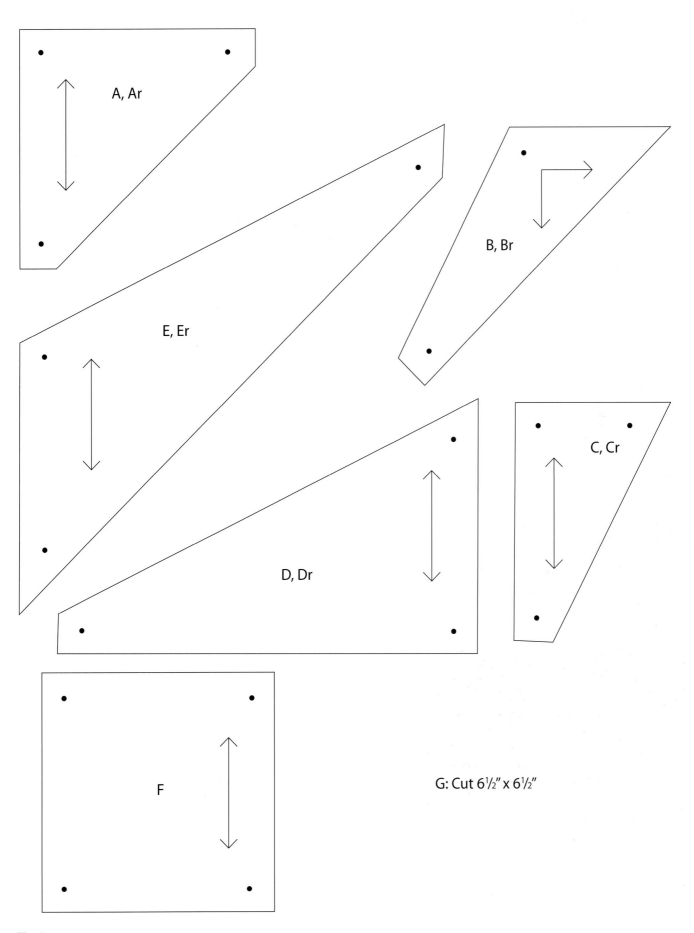

A, Ar

E, Er

B, Br

C, Cr

D, Dr

F

G: Cut 6½" x 6½"

Fig. 5.

Karen's photo by Alice A. McWilliams

Finalist
Karen Watts
Houston, Texas

I started quilting in 1991, thinking I would "just make one." It was a sampler, made by tracing around cardboard templates and cutting out the pieces with scissors. I didn't know there was such a thing as a rotary cutter! The entire process of constructing a quilt immediately appealed to me and I have been obsessively making quilts since. For years I made quilts using established patterns, but with unusual or bright colors.

It has been only recently that I discovered the fun of designing my own quilts. I belong to a bee that has been together for 10 years now. We call ourselves Kindred Spirits. When we first started meeting we did block exchanges and challenged ourselves to figure out a unique way to set our blocks. Next we did a portrait exchange. We called our next challenge the Page 36 Challenge. We each brought in a non-quilting magazine. We drew for the magazines and had another drawing to determine a page number—it was 36. Everyone had to turn to page 36 and make a quilt that was inspired in some way by what was on it. We exhibited our challenges at our guild's quilt shows and they were very well received. Sometimes we have a size limitation, but our bee's most famous rule is, "There are no rules!"

My quilt guild, Lakeview Quilters Guild, entered the AQS Ultimate Guild Challenge in 2005 and 2007. We were so excited to win first place in 2007 with our theme of "fruit." I had a quilt in each exhibit and had a lot of fun making each one.

I started out with the smallest upstairs bedroom as my sewing room, and that has expanded to two downstairs rooms that were intended by the builder to be the formal living and dining rooms. Who needed those? One is now my sewing room with a large design wall, and the other is the quilting room with my Gammill machine in it. People coming in the front door know immediately that they are in the home of a quilter. I have two children and became a stay-at-home mom in 1992, when my youngest was six months old. Quilting and being involved in the bee and our guild was a way to stay sane and connected with the adult world. We all agree, quilting is much cheaper than therapy.

My goals for quilting in the future definitely include the next MAQS contest. I have already started playing around with designs for Burgoyne Surrounded and will have a hard time deciding which one to make. Like most quilters, I have ideas for more quilts than I could possibly make in my lifetime, but I'll certainly give it my best shot!

SAWTOOTH SPIN 56" x 56"

*I simply love color. I've learned that a simple quilt
pattern can be spectacular with an innovative use of color.*

Inspiration & Design

I have enjoyed the quilts in the New Quilts from an Old Favorite books from the beginning but never really thought to make one until I saw the 2007 block. The Sawtooth block looks Southwestern to me, and since I love Southwestern designs, I had to try to design a quilt for the contest.

I recently bought Electric Quilt® 6 software and had just gone through their tutorials, so I decided to attempt an original design using the software. I quickly found out that there are two challenging things about EQ6. One, you can design dozens of quilts and color them all differently, but then you have to decide which one to make. Two, you can easily design quilts that may be quite difficult to sew. I ran into both of these situations. There are almost 30 Sawtooth designs with variations in my folder and the one I chose was definitely not easy! I think I did more ripping out on this quilt than on any other I've made.

When I finally chose which design I liked best, I colored it on the computer in many different ways. I discovered that splitting the block in half diagonally and coloring the backgrounds differently gave me the spinning design in the center, as well as the center square behind it. I really liked the transparency effect with the Double Sawtooth blocks and the center spinning blocks (fig. 1).

After trying several color palettes, I chose the chocolate brown, gold, and silver colorway. I love the silvery gray fabric in the center, and chose the mottled gold background fabric to complement it. The fabric for the points of the corner and Double Sawtooth blocks has a wonderful texture that reminds me of sandstone. The circle print used in the center of the corner squares tied it all together (fig. 2).

Although I have been using a lot of batiks lately, this quilt has only commercially printed fabric in it and almost all of it was already in my stash.

The biggest challenge in making this quilt was constructing the stretched Sawtooth blocks. They look like diamonds, but are actually parallelograms—two of the sides are just about $^3/_8$" longer than the other two (fig. 3).

I really had to pay attention when I was paper piecing the points that I was using the correct points, as the four sides were not identical. Then, sewing all the blocks together while trying to match all the points was a challenge as well! I originally thought there would be many set-in seams, but I soon realized I could divide the top into quarters diagonally and piece it with no set-in seams at all.

Fig. 1.

Fig. 2.

Choosing a border design and making it fit was another challenge. All in all, I think facing these challenges improved my skills, and I'm looking forward to the next one.

Technique

Probably the most useful technique I used in this quilt was paper piecing. On this quilt I used some tips and techniques that I learned from Judy Niemeyer and Susan Garman. These tips are especially useful for piecing unusual shapes like the skewed points on the stretched Sawtooth blocks.

Precut your fabric to the general shape of the finished piece, adding a generous seam allowance. I add ⅜" and rough cut them. The pieces do not need to be precise. This allows you to place them more accurately when sewing and also reduces waste of fabric, which can happen if you use strips for your paper piecing.

When adding pieces to your paper pattern, sew to the finished line of the piece; that is, do not sew into the seam allowance or cross a previously stitched line. If you are using tiny stitches they will not pull out. This allows for easier paper removal and also enables you to use the next tip.

After sewing a piece to the paper, open the fabric and press it. Now, before adding the next fabric piece, fold back the paper on the next stitching line. You will see the seam allowance of the piece just sewn hanging over, and since you have cut generous-sized pieces, the seam allowance will be more than $^1/_4$". Trim it to $^1/_4$". Now you can easily line up the next piece with the trimmed edge without having to guess at the proper alignment. If I am adding a light fabric to a dark one, I trim the seam allowance to slightly less than $^1/_4$" and make sure I completely cover the dark seam allowance with the light fabric piece. This eliminates shadowing on the front of the block.

Some other good general tips for making paper piecing fast and efficient are:

Use a tiny stitch when piecing your fabric to the paper as it makes removing the paper easier. Remember to set your stitch length back to normal when sewing your paper-pieced units together.

Remove the paper before sewing units to each other for two reasons: it is easier to make sure points match, etc., and it's one less seam line to worry about when removing the paper.

Match your thread color to your background. If you are using a dark background, use a dark thread. I have seen many quilts that show light thread on dark fabric paper-pieced units after they have been pressed open. You don't want to see dark thread on light fabric either.

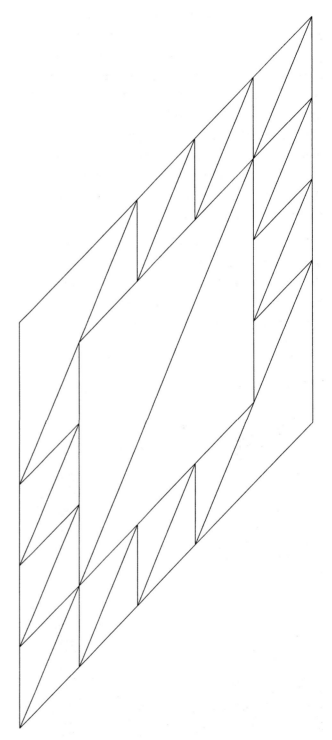

Fig. 3.

Sandra's photo by David P. Werlich

Finalist
Sandra Werlich
Carbondale, Illinois

My brief introduction to sewing came in one segment of a high-school home economics class. My mother disliked sewing and avoided it. But I had heard stories about the depression of the 1930s, when my grandmother made clothes for the entire family out of economic necessity. As a young wife and mother in the 1960s, I turned to sewing, also to save money, but primarily because I couldn't find attractive, affordable maternity clothes. I continued making my own clothes as well as many things for my children (and even for my husband) until I began working full time, several years later. Thereafter, I kept my hands busy during my limited spare time with knitting and cross-stitching. Only occasionally did I return to my sewing machine to make items that I could not find in stores.

As retirement approached after 25 years in retail management, I tried my hand at quilting. A few quilt kits got me started. I celebrated my ultimate liberation with the purchase of a good sewing machine and cabinet. My first "real" quilts were a pair of Dresden Plate quilts for some new twin beds. These turned out so well that I was soon taking custom orders from my children and grandchildren for bed covers and throws—whimsical creations featuring reptiles, insects, and trucks. And each new addition to our extended family received a baby quilt from Aunt Sandra. I was hooked on quilting.

Full-sized quilts required too much time, however, leaving insufficient opportunity to explore my ideas. So I tried art quilting. I had always enjoyed arts and crafts. I had a fair knack for drawing and my work in floral design provided experience with composition. Considerable travel over the years sharpened my eye and heightened my aesthetic sensibilities.

My first two art quilts were selected for shows, the second one earning a prize, and several others have since received recognition. My quilts have become increasingly more complex, often suggesting movement. Several of my works have whimsical themes, but most are nature-based, with flora as a special favorite. I prefer vibrant colors, but have also dabbled in pastels and even experimented with a chromatically minimalist piece in black, white, and gray.

SAWTOOTH GARDEN 62" x 56½"

I welcomed an invitation to join an art quilt group in my community whose very experienced and successful members have encouraged my development as a quilter.

Fig. 1.

Inspiration & Design

I was apprehensive when the five members of my art quilt group decided to enter the MAQS New Quilts from an Old Favorite contest. I had not worked with this block before but I soon determined that an appropriate subject would be one of my old familiar favorites—flowers. I had several years experience as a floral designer and I love gardening, too, especially the design of flower beds. I mentally selected floral species with natural sawtooth shapes. With a "basket" of these images, I designed my quilt as I would a substantial bouquet, a large centerpiece arrangement, and ultimately a SAWTOOTH GARDEN. I found the flowers in my own garden and a local park. The design involved decisions about shape, size, color, and placement for a balanced composition.

Fortunately, I found most of the necessary fabrics in my stash and soon my sewing machine and I were transforming imagination into reality. My friends in the art quilt group provided useful critiques and much encouragement.

I "planted" my garden with coneflowers (Echinacea), blanket flowers (Gaillardia), and ferns. All are jaggedy-edged species with enough natural variation for an attractive, interesting quilt. Bright-colored, zigzag stitching added interest, especially while carrying the contest theme to the dark soil (figs. 1–3).

Fig. 2.

Technique

I began with a full-size sketch, modifying it several times. When I was satisfied with the design, I divided the finished drawing into sections, outlining these with a black felt-tipped marker. Then I traced the sections with their component parts onto the dull side of freezer paper. Hash lines were added to indicate connecting seams. The several sections were labeled alphabetically and their components were numbered in piecing order to create a coded pattern. For the more complex sections, I also added references for the fabrics to be used. To aid in piecing, I photocopied the more complicated sections of this map.

Working in sections, I cut the coded pattern pieces from the freezer paper and ironed each of these onto its assigned fabric. Then I cut the pieces from the fabrics, adding a quarter-inch seam allowance before removing the paper. After piecing and sewing a few sections together, I attached the other sections as they were completed.

The most enjoyable part of the entire project was the auditioning of various fabrics for the quilt. As the design took shape, I culled through my stash of cotton fabrics, narrowing the possibilities for the various elements. I pinned swatches onto the original drawing, now mounted on a large, foam-core board, to find the best combinations of colors and patterns. From the beginning I knew that I wanted a background of black fabric to make the colorful flowers pop. I wanted the quilting to be whimsical, like the garden itself. So I chose (what else?) zigzag stitches, using a variety of colorful rayon, polyester, and neon threads.

Fig. 3.

SAWTOOTH BLOCK PATTERNS

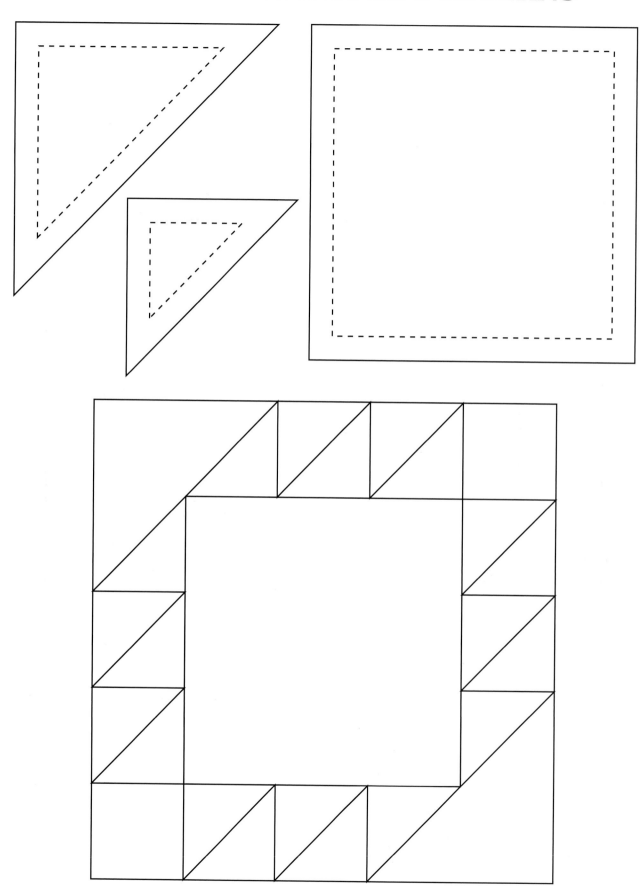

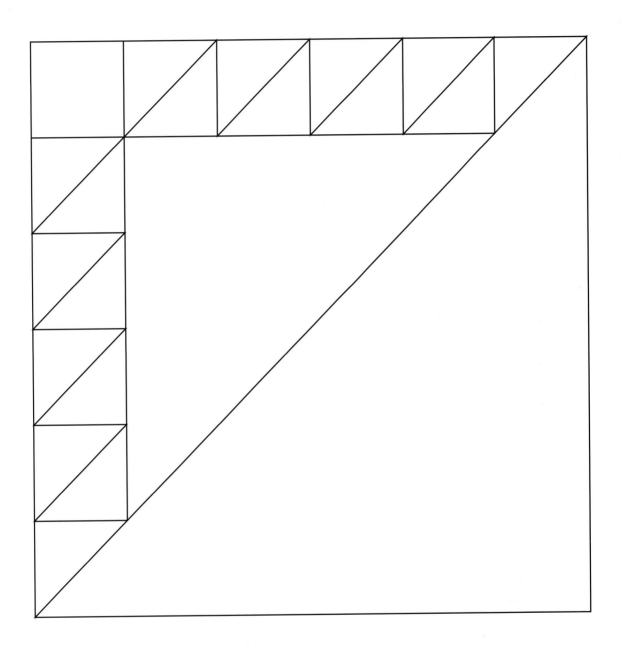

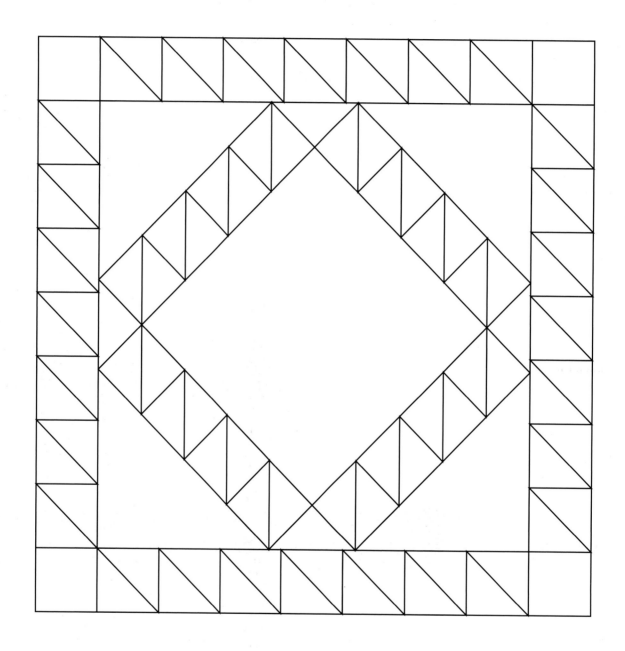

Sᴀᴡᴛᴏᴏᴛʜ: New Quilts from an Old Favorite

RESOURCES

Books

Adam, Cheryl A., *Off Center Patchwork*. Paducah, Kentucky: American Quilter's Society, 2003.

Barber, Barbara. *Foolproof Curves: Quilts with Bias Strips and Continuous Paper Piecing*. Concord, California: C&T Publishing, 2004.

Brackman, Barbara. *Encyclopedia of Quilt Patterns*. Paducah, Kentucky: American Quilter's Society, 1993.

Marston, Gwen. *Liberated Quiltmaking*. Paducah, Kentucky: American Quilter's Society, 1997.

McCloskey, Marsha. *Marsha McCloskey's Block Party: A Quilter's Extravaganza of 120 Rotary-Block Patterns*. Emmaus, Pennsylvania: Rodale Books, 2000.

Schamber, Sharon and Cristy Fincher. *Piece by Piece: Machine Appliqué*. Paducah, Kentucky: American Quilter's Society, 2007.

Smith, Loretta. *Pineapple Quilt: A Piece of Cake*. San Marcos, California: Quilt in a Day, 1989.

Software

Adobe® Illustrator®
www.adobe.com

Custom Fibonacci Spiral Generator by Ned May
chromatism.net/cfsg.htm

Electric Quilt®
www.electricquilt.com

Hola Mola, embroidery designs by Nancy Vasilchik
www.sewbiz.biz

Web Sites

Great Lakes Quilt Center
museum.msu.edu/glqc/index.html

International Quilt Study Center
www.quiltstudy.org

Jane A. Sassaman
www.janeasassaman.com

Libby Lehman
www.libbylehman.us

Quilt Index
www.quiltindex.org

Ruth B. McDowell
www.Ruthbmcdowell.com

Southern Highland Craft Guild
www.southernhighlandguild.org

Fabrics

Caryl Bryer Fallert
www.bryerpatch.com

RaNae Merrill Quilt Design
www.ranaemerrillquilts.com

Wendy Richardson
www.QTStudio.com

The National Quilt Museum, Museum of the American Quilter's Society, is the world's largest and foremost museum devoted to quilts and the only museum dedicated to today's quilts and quiltmakers. Established in 1991 by AQS founders Bill and Meredith Schroeder as a not-for-profit organization, the museum is located in a 27,000 square-foot facility. It was designed specifically to display quilts effectively and safely. Three expansive galleries envelop visitors in color, exquisite stitchery, and design.

The highlight of any visit is The William & Meredith Schroeder Gallery, with a rotating installation of quilts from the museum's permanent collection of over 300 quilts. Before the museum opened, the Schroeders had acquired a private collection of remarkable quilts. In addition to being a source of wonder for the owners, the collection came to recognize extraordinary contemporary quilts and their makers. Through the Schroeders' generosity, the nucleus of the museum's collection was formed. In addition, the permanent collection includes award-winning quilts from the annual AQS Quilt Show & Contest. In 2006, "Oh, Wow!"—a stunning collection of more than 40 miniature quilts—was added to the collection. Educational programs offered in three well-equipped classrooms serve local and national audiences. The museum offers an annual schedule of in-depth workshops taught by master quilters. Children and families can participate in hands-on projects. Exhibitions developed by MAQS, like New Quilts from an Old Favorite, travel to other galleries and museums, helping to educate and inspire a wider spectrum of viewers. With more than 1000 quilt-related book titles available, the museum's bookstore has one of the largest selections of quilt books anywhere. In addition, the museum's shop offers special quilt-related

Photos by Jessica Byassee

American Quilter's Society
(MAQS)

merchandise as well as fine crafts by artisans from this region and beyond. The entire facility is wheelchair accessible.

Located at 215 Jefferson Street in historic downtown Paducah, Kentucky, the museum is open year-round 10 A.M. to 5 P.M., Monday through Saturday. From April 1 through October 31, it is also open Sundays from 1 to 5 P.M. For extended hours during special events such as the AQS Quilt Show & Contest, please check the museum's Web site listed below.

The museum programs can also be sampled on the Web site: www.quiltmuseum.org.
For more information,
e-mail: info@quiltmuseum.org
call: (270) 442-8856
or write: MAQS
PO Box 1540
Paducah, KY 42002-1540

OTHER AQS BOOKS

This is only a small selection of the books available from the American Quilter's Society. AQS books are known worldwide for timely topics, clear writing, beautiful color photos, and accurate illustrations and patterns. The following books are available from your local bookseller, quilt shop, or public library.

#7074   US$22.95

#6899   US$21.95

#7600   US$26.95

#7605   US$24.95

#7601   US$26.95

#7609   US$19.95

#7079   US$22.95

#7491   US$22.95

#7484   US$22.95

Look for these books nationally.
Call or **Visit** our Web site at

1-800-626-5420
www.AmericanQuilter.com